Cha

BREAKING BAD HABITS IN PARROTS

HOW RESPONSIBLE AND SYMPATHETIC PARROT CARE
CAN PREVENT OR REMEDY PROBLEM BEHAVIORS

BREAKING
BAD
HABITS
IN
PARROTS

FIREFLY BOOKS

Acknowledgments
Greg would like to thank Rachel Lewis for her comments on the text. Red, Martha, Mr. Big and Jasper performed to their usual high standards.

For Interpet Publishing
Editor Philip de Ste. Croix
Designer Philip Clucas MCDS
Photographer Neil Sutherland
Diagram artwork Martin Reed
Index Amanda O'Neill
Production management Consortium, Suffolk

A FIREFLY BOOK

Published by Firefly Books Ltd. 2007

First printing

Publisher Cataloging-in-Publication Data (U.S.)
Glendell, Greg, 1953–
    Breaking bad habits in parrots: how sympathetic and responsible parrot care can prevent or remedy common problem behavior / Greg Glendell.
[128] p. : col. photos. ;   cm.
Includes index.
Summary: Describes how to keep a parrot in a domestic environment, and techniques to overcome problem behaviors, such as screaming, self-plucking, biting, aggression and destructive habits.
ISBN-13: 978-1-55407-297-2
ISBN-10: 1-55407-297-2
    1. Parrots—Behavior. I. Title.
636.6865 dc22   SF473.P3.G546 2007

Library and Archives Canada Cataloguing in Publication
Glendell, Greg, 1953–
    Breaking bad habits in parrots : how sympathetic and responsible parrot care can prevent or remedy common problem behaviors / Greg Glendell.
Includes index.
ISBN-13: 978-1-55407-297-2
ISBN-10: 1-55407-297-2
    1. Parrots—Behavior. 2. Parrots—Training. I. Title.
SF473.P3G54 2007   636.6'865   C2007-902634-6

Published in the United States by
Firefly Books (U.S.) Inc.
P.O. Box 1338, Ellicott Station
Buffalo, New York 14205

Published in Canada by
Firefly Books Ltd.
66 Leek Crescent
Richmond Hill, Ontario L4B 1H1

Printed in China

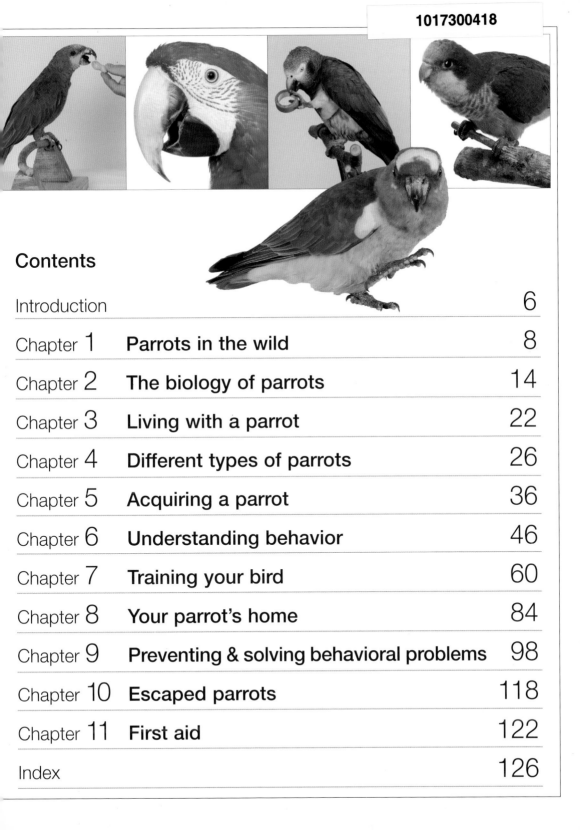

Contents

Introduction   6

Chapter 1   **Parrots in the wild**   8

Chapter 2   **The biology of parrots**   14

Chapter 3   **Living with a parrot**   22

Chapter 4   **Different types of parrots**   26

Chapter 5   **Acquiring a parrot**   36

Chapter 6   **Understanding behavior**   46

Chapter 7   **Training your bird**   60

Chapter 8   **Your parrot's home**   84

Chapter 9   **Preventing & solving behavioral problems**   98

Chapter 10   **Escaped parrots**   118

Chapter 11   **First aid**   122

Index   126

Introduction

This book is intended for pet or "companion" parrot owners. It is meant to a be a practical book that gives you, as a parrot-keeper, the information you need to fully understand your bird's behavior, whatever type of parrot you may have.

In addition to giving detailed guidance on how to develop an excellent relationship with your pet bird, the book gives an insight into parrots' natural behaviors and how these birds live in the wild. There are details of the "language" of parrots—the calls and postures the birds use—and how to interpret these behaviors. The essentials of behavior and, most importantly, what motivates a bird to perform the range of behaviors we see in them, is explained. While the use of proven scientific methods for understanding and changing behaviors is covered in detail, again the aim is for this to be of practical benefit to you as a pet-bird-keeper. This leads to a section that considers how you can use these methods to work with your bird, both to prevent problems in the future and to solve any current problems you may be experiencing. Problem behaviors such as nervousness, aggression, self-plucking, excessive screaming and destructiveness are all covered. Once you understand the causes of problem behaviors, these can usually be solved by working with your bird's innate intelligence to ask it to change its behavior.

The importance of allowing pet parrots to perform as many of their natural behaviors as possible in captivity is emphasized, and this is supported by details of how you can provide environmental enrichment for the birds. Unlike other pet parrot books, there is no assumption here that parrots should be wing-clipped. More people want to keep their birds as the flying creatures they are meant to be, so this book explains in detail how to teach pet birds basic flight commands. This ensures that you have a well-behaved parrot that can also be encouraged to fly.

If you want to teach your bird to talk, the book suggests you encourage the use of words and phrases in their proper context, just as you might to encourage a human toddler to talk. This allows you to develop a much better level of communication with your bird. There are also sections on how to recover a bird that may have escaped, and details of what to do in an emergency to provide first aid care for your bird.

Breaking Bad Habits in Parrots offers a new and refreshing approach to keeping parrots so that both you and your bird can get more out of each other's company. Birds are fascinating creatures and the parrot group, in particular, have unique qualities. Keeping parrots as pets is a real privilege. This book aims to give you a revealing insight into your parrot's life.

Above: *A scarlet macaw. Like all parrots, macaws are highly intelligent birds with a complex set of needs.*
Right: *Parrots' beauty is best appreciated when seeing them in flight, like this pair of blue and gold macaws.*

Parrots in the wild

Many companion animals, such as dogs and cats, have been domesticated for thousands of years. Some types are bred for particular temperamental characteristics, with some being more docile than others. But parrots, even hand-reared ones bred in captivity, are very different. With very few possible exceptions, such as budgerigars (commonly called parakeets) and cockatiels, parrots cannot be described as domesticated creatures. Although they are companion or "pet" birds, all parrots retain all their "wild-type" behaviors and behavioral needs. This section looks at how parrots live in the wild. Understanding something about their natural lives will give you a better insight into their needs in captivity.

SAFETY IN NUMBERS

All parrots are vulnerable to predators such as hawks and other animals. To reduce the threat of becoming another creature's meal, parrots have developed two important behavioral traits. Firstly, parrots are highly social creatures and live in groups, often quite large flocks. This gives them better protection from predators, since there are many eyes looking out for potential dangers. Secondly, they have a highly developed repertoire of calls and postures, which make up their "language." This language gives parrots a means of communicating with each other. They can inform one another of different types of threat, such as flying predators or those on the ground, and if or when they need to flee or to hide from them. Other calls are used to keep in mutual contact or to signal when it is time to fly to a feeding area or go to roost.

COMMUNICATION SKILLS

Parrots can recognize many members of their own flock as individuals, and each bird may be able to distinguish hundreds of other birds.
Much of the birds' repertoire is used to minimize aggression within the flock. While there will

Above: *Green-winged macaws. Like most parrots, these birds live in groups that are often very large. Their habitat may cover many square miles.*

CHAPTER 1

Above: *These cockatoos are having a minor dispute. The birds' "language" and postures are used to minimize demonstrations of actual physical aggression.*

certainly be some birds in the flock that are more confident than others, parrots do not have a simple pecking order, as you might see in a flock of domestic hens. They use their language to show both their reactions to things going on around them and their intentions toward each other. Using the calls and postures of their language also helps greatly to reduce aggression within the flock, and serious fighting occurs very rarely in wild birds. Most species also enjoy a plentiful supply of food, so parrots rarely need to squabble over this.

However, where nesting sites are hard to find, fighting can occur.

Wild parrots have complete freedom to go wherever they wish, and as part of their normal behavior many birds fly hundreds of miles every week as they travel between food sources, roosting sites and nesting sites. Some species, such as budgerigars and some cockatoos, are nomadic. These birds will roost in a different site every few days as they explore new areas for food or nesting sites. Other species, such as African grays and most Amazon parrots, are more sedentary and have favorite feeding sites within a large, but defined, territorial area.

The importance of flight

The importance of flight to parrots, including companion birds, cannot be overemphasized. Parrots have spent millions of years evolving into perfect flying creatures, and their whole lifestyle and biology has developed around being able to fly. Every part of a bird's body—such as its lightweight bones, strong but very light feathers, the huge muscles in its chest and relatively massive heart—are designed to enable it to fly at considerable speeds with the minimum of effort. Parrots, therefore, live in a more three-dimensional world than most mammals, like ourselves, who remain on the ground.

Above: *Parrots fly at around 40 mph (60 km/h), and they can travel huge distances easily and rapidly each day as they seek out their favorite foods in the forest.*

BORN TO FLY!
The ability to fly affects the birds' attitude to the heights of all the things in their environment. Food sources that are down low or on the ground present a greater risk to the birds than food found in the treetops, where parrots are generally very safe. Nesting holes that are too low will not be used, and a hawk overhead is far more dangerous than the same hawk flying below a group of parrots.

Like all flying birds, parrots have an instinctive escape reflex action that is used to avoid being preyed upon. As it's a reflex action, the bird has little control of it once it takes place. It is much the same as your reflex action that causes you to snatch your hand away from a hot surface before getting burned; it happens in a fraction of a second. The bird's escape reflex action results in the bird taking to the air immediately if it feels under serious threat from some other creature or action. The parrot will then fly as fast as it can away from the threat until it is safe. Flying at 35 to 50 miles per hour (55 to 80 km/h) allows parrots to escape most predators if they see them in time. Pet birds retain this reflex escape reaction, even if they have been wing-clipped, since (by definition) a reflex action is not under the bird's voluntary control. So wing-clipped birds can be vulnerable to crash landings on hard surfaces.

Parrots can see far more colors than humans. In addition to the colors that we can see (mixtures of red, green and blue light only), parrots can see ultraviolet light, probably as a separate color that we cannot conceive. Humans have three different types of color receptors in their eyes, which correspond to the three main colors we can see. Most birds have four types of these receptors, including the UV type. So, some birds, such as African gray parrots, which appear to us to be simply gray birds with a red tail, may in fact have many colors that humans cannot

see, and appear as brilliantly colored birds to their own kind. Parrots also have an extremely well-developed sense of hearing and may be

able to hear sounds beyond our range of hearing, just as dogs can hear ultra-sonic sounds. They may also be able to produce sounds that we cannot hear.

UNDERSTANDING YOUR BIRD'S NEEDS

Just consider how different companion parrots' lives are from their wild relations. Many pet parrots have to cope with being in a cage; they

Above: *Galahs form huge flocks in Australia, where they are considered a pest in wheat-growing areas.*
Left: *In just half an hour this cockatoo could be 20 m. (30 km) away feeding on some other type of food.*

fly very little, if at all, and the time they spend in the company of other birds or humans is often very restricted. However, parrots are highly intelligent and, given suitable care from a knowledgeable owner, most can adapt to live contentedly in captivity. But to have success in this, the carer must develop a very good knowledge of their bird's needs, particularly the behavioral needs.

Daytime activities

Since captive birds are kept in cages or aviaries, the casual observer might assume that parrots are not particularly active. However, that would be far from the truth. Captive parrots' movements are simply restricted as a result of their housing conditions. In the wild, parrots are highly active creatures. As with most other birds, flight allows parrots to move at speeds and over distances that other animals cannot achieve. Wild parrots may have a wide range of feeding sites separated by dozens, even hundreds, of miles. Being able to fly at speeds similar to human commuters means that birds can cover many

miles during a flight of less than an hour. A flock of parrots may leave their roosting site in the morning and commute to their first feeding area, which could be more than 20 miles (30 km) away, but it would only take them half an hour to arrive. They may use many feeding sites throughout the day, feeding on a wide range of fruits, seeds, nuts, leaves and flowers, depending on the species' preferences. They appear to be quite wasteful feeders and seem to enjoy stripping twigs, bark and unwanted bits of fruits and seeds off their feeding trees. This activity may induce the trees to produce more fruits or seeds in succeeding years.

SOWING SEEDS FOR THE FUTURE

Parrots are also unwitting agents who distribute the seeds of some of their feed trees. Any undigested seeds are excreted, often far from the feeding site, and some of these produce new trees for future generations of birds. Some parrots also take minerals from "clay licks" (cliff-side areas of bare soil) or descend to the ground to eat certain types of soils to aid their digestion or neutralize any toxins in their bodies. Many tropical rain forest parrots do not need to drink water as their food contains all the fluids they need. But birds from arid regions in some African countries and Australia do need to find water on most days.

Above: *This African brown-headed parrot eats a wide range of foods including, as shown here, flowers.*
Above top: *Some parrots, such as this rainbow lorikeet, depend on nectar as their main source of food.*

Parrots in the wild

during these bathing sessions. These showers are vital for keeping the birds' feathers in tip-top condition. Birds with poor feather quality fly less well and have poor protection from the cold, and even in the tropics, where most parrots come from, nights can sometimes be cold. Pet parrots need to be showered regularly to replicate this feather-conditioning activity.

Wild parrots are highly active birds and lead busy lives, socializing with their flock mates throughout the day. It is only at night, once they have gone to roost, that they settle down to rest and are then reluctant to fly again until dawn.

Left: *Galahs live in semidesert habitats and need to find water on most days.*
Below: *Many parrots, such as these blue-headed pionus parrots and mealy Amazons, eat soil at clay licks. This helps them to digest other foods.*

DAY-TO-DAY ACTIVITIES

Other daily activities include bathing, preening and having an afternoon siesta—most parrots prefer to spend the hottest part of the day deep in the shade of trees, where they can have a snooze in safety. While some parrots do bathe in water, most birds actually take a shower. This is done during heavy downpours, when the birds fluff out their feathers as they try to get as wet as they can in the rain. They will also roll around in trees, hanging upside down, rubbing themselves on the leaves and generally playing around

The biology of parrots

Birds are a very large group of animals, with over 9,000 species—twice as many species as mammals. There are 333 species of parrots, and these range from tiny parrotlets, no bigger than a sparrow, to macaws as big as an eagle with a 5-foot (1.5 m) wingspan. Despite this great range in sizes, all parrots have a very similar body-plan, which is constructed on a lightweight but strong skeleton.

THE SKELETON

Like most birds, parrots are highly adapted for flying and everything about their design is aimed at making flight as efficient as possible. But parrots spend as much time in the trees or on the ground as they do flying, so the skeleton has to serve both the needs of flight and the needs of a highly active, climbing animal. As a result, the skeleton is a compromise between these two methods of getting around, but it serves them very well.

Parrots have light, hollow, often air-filled bones that are very strong for their weight.

State-of-the-art airframe
In the course of evolution the demands for efficient flight have stripped out any unnecessary weight from every bone in a flying bird's body. The skeleton of some birds is so light that it weighs less than the bird's own feathers.

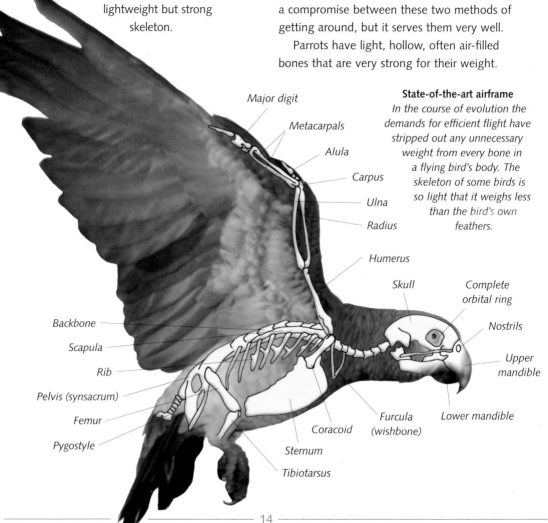

Major digit
Metacarpals
Alula
Carpus
Ulna
Radius
Humerus
Skull
Complete orbital ring
Nostrils
Upper mandible
Backbone
Scapula
Rib
Pelvis (synsacrum)
Femur
Pygostyle
Coracoid
Furcula (wishbone)
Lower mandible
Sternum
Tibiotarsus

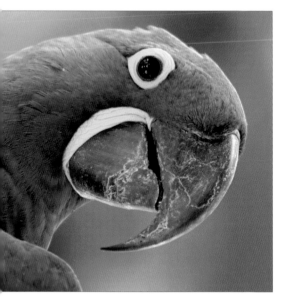

Above: *Macaws, like this hyacinth, have huge bills that are easily capable of breaking open Brazil nuts.*

During their evolution they have dispensed with any unnecessary bones and, like all birds, have lost all teeth. Many bones are fused together to reduce weight yet retain the strength needed for flight. Most of the bones in the back are fused so the bird's spine is a rigid rod that acts, much like the frame of an aircraft's fuselage, as the main support for the powerful wings. In a parrot's spine, only the neck and one joint in the tail are movable, but their necks are so flexible that they can reach almost all parts of their bodies to preen their feathers. The ribs hang off the spine and support the huge shield-shaped breastbone, or sternum. The relative size and shape of this bone is unique to birds. With its projecting "keel" it provides a large area to which the wing muscles are attached.

GETTING TO GRIPS WITH FOOD

Birds have reduced "fingers", with only three rudimentary digits remaining in the wing tips. Although parrots' legs appear quite short, they have a surprisingly long stride. This helps them to climb around in trees with ease. The skull is large, and the most notable features are the huge eye sockets and large braincase; parrots are very reliant on sight for all their daily activities. The visible part of the beak is made of keratin, the same material that's in our hair and nails, and this is continually growing from within at a slow rate. It is supported by bone underneath. The bill is used as an extra grasping "hand" when the bird is climbing around in trees. This means that parrots can easily climb out to the ends of branches to reach fruits, buds and seeds without having to hover near them as other birds do. To ensure a strong grip on branches, all parrots from budgerigars to macaws have the same type of foot: it has four toes, with two facing backward and two facing forward. This arrangement is found in other climbing birds, such as woodpeckers. Most parrots also use their feet as we use our hands, and they can hold and manipulate food or other small objects in their feet and put these up to their beak to take them apart.

Right: *This Timneh gray holds a peanut in its right foot so that it can deftly extract the nuts one at a time.*

Muscles—the powerhouse for flight

All a bird's major muscles are anchored onto the skeleton, and it is the flight muscles that are the parrot's most important means of propulsion. While the wings themselves only have small muscles used to make adjustments during flight, the main muscles used to propel the bird in flight are the pectorals. They are attached to the sternum and have tendons attaching them to the wings. These flight muscles alone can account for around 30 percent of a parrot's weight. Muscles at the bottom of the spine move the tail in all directions to aid steering and "braking" when the bird comes in to land.

MUSCLES FOR AN ACTIVE LIFE

The muscles for walking are situated high up in the legs, above the knee, and this ensures they are located at the center of gravity when the bird is walking. The waddling gait of birds is due to their inflexible spines. So when walking, they have to transfer all their weight over each leg with

Above: *Parrots can raise and lower most of their feathers at will. Cockatoos have developed this ability with large erectile crests.*
Left: *The powerful muscles that articulate the bill enable parrots to crack open hard nuts.*

each stride to maintain good balance. The other major muscle is, of course, the heart, located within the rib cage slightly to the left-hand side. Birds' hearts operate at a much faster rate than human hearts. Even at rest a small parrot's heart will be beating at around 140 times a minute—twice the rate of the human heart. However, while in flight a parrot's heart will be beating at around 1,000 times a minute.

The biology of parrots

Above: *A bird's rigid spine means it walks with a waddling stride, rolling from side to side with each step.*

feathers. Some parrots, such as cockatoos, have large erectile crests, and these are powered by muscles attached to the forehead behind the nostrils. Parrots have a very strong crushing power in their bills, which is needed for breaking into hard seeds and nuts and for excavating their nesting holes in trees and soft rocks. Though rarely used in serious fighting, the beak can be a formidable weapon if a bird feels threatened, and parrots are capable of killing other birds.

Birds need to be able to raise and lower their feathers for a range of reasons, including heat regulation and displaying to other birds. Countless tiny muscles are found throughout the skin at the base of most of the

Extensors

Flexi cardiulnaris

Pronator longus

Brachioradialis

Extensor carpi radialis

Triceps

Latissimus dorsi

Sartorius

Ilio tibialis

Ilio fibularis

Biceps

Gastrocnemius

Muscles for flight
The powerhouse for fast, efficient flight lies in the huge pectoral muscles in the chest area.

Pectorals

Peroneus

Feathers—for warmth & for flight

While many animals have hair and scales, feathers are unique to birds, and they allow them to fly with great efficiency. Feathers also act as a highly efficient insulating layer to help maintain

Above: *The feather coloring develops as each one grows, but colors can change or fade slightly with wear.*

the birds' very high body temperature. Feathers also give birds the typical streamlined bullet-shaped body that greatly reduces wind resistance during flight. There is a long-running debate among scientists as to whether birds developed feathers before they became warm-blooded or while they still had most of their reptilian scales and were cold-blooded, but these two developments could have arisen together.

DIFFERENT TYPES OF FEATHERS

Feathers are made of keratin, the same substance that constitutes the bird's beak. Parrots have a fluffy undercoat of soft down feathers, plus some hairlike "filoplumes" and sensory hairlike feathers around the eyes and nostrils. But most feathers comprise the main body-covering contour feathers and of course the large flight feathers attached to the wings and tail. Most parrots have nine or ten primary feathers; these are the largest, outermost wing feathers, attached to the bird's "hand". They also have 12 secondary feathers that are attached to the forearm. The tail usually comprises 12 feathers.

One group of parrots, the conures from South America that range in size from a budgerigar to a small macaw, have long stiff tails they use as a prop when climbing around in trees, again similar to woodpeckers. This means these birds do not have to use their beaks as much as other parrots for climbing. The structure of feathers is easily revealed with a good magnifying glass, which shows that this very lightweight but strong body covering is far more complex than the hairs or scales found on other creatures. Each feather has

Left: *Some parrots, such as this scarlet macaw, have bare white facial skin patches. These turn red when a bird flushes with excitement.*

Far left: *The right wing of a Meyer's parrot showing the primary flight feathers. Primary feather number 9 is a blood feather and still growing down.*

The biology of parrots

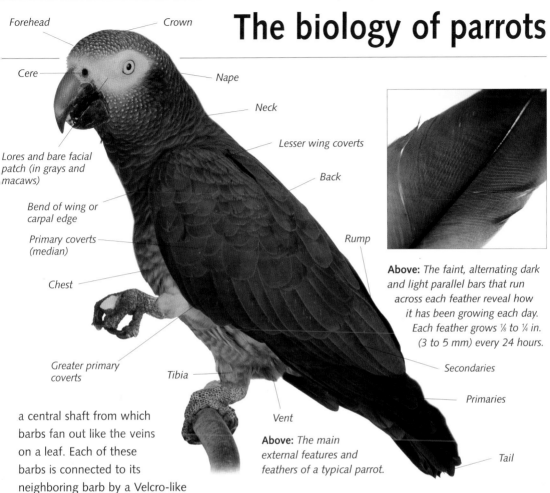

Forehead

Crown

Cere

Nape

Neck

Lesser wing coverts

Lores and bare facial patch (in grays and macaws)

Back

Bend of wing or carpal edge

Primary coverts (median)

Rump

Chest

Greater primary coverts

Tibia

Secondaries

Primaries

Vent

Tail

Above: *The faint, alternating dark and light parallel bars that run across each feather reveal how it has been growing each day. Each feather grows ⅛ to ¼ in. (3 to 5 mm) every 24 hours.*

Above: *The main external features and feathers of a typical parrot.*

a central shaft from which barbs fan out like the veins on a leaf. Each of these barbs is connected to its neighboring barb by a Velcro-like arrangement of hooks and pegs. Although they can be separated fairly easily, they can also be zipped up again very quickly as the bird bathes, shakes itself and preens.

FEATHER CARE
Parrots spend a good deal of time preening their feathers. In the wild, most parrots also get drenched with water by daily rain showers, and this too is vital to help maintain and condition feathers. Captive parrots need to be sprayed frequently with a fine mist of plain water to replicate the daily shower they would get in the

wild. The main flight feathers are extremely strong and remarkably rigid as arranged in the wings. Feathers have a limited life and need to be replaced regularly. Parrots usually molt their feathers once a year, and the process takes longer in larger birds than in small species. An African gray or Amazon parrot will take seven to nine months to replace all of its feathers completely, but smaller birds, such as lovebirds and cockatiels, may only take two or three months. Some of the larger birds, such as macaws and cockatoos, take much more than a year to complete a molt. As a result, parrots actually spend more time molting than not molting.

Finding & consuming food

Wild parrots are highly mobile creatures. This mobility allows them to range over a huge area of their habitat for food. Different types of food (different species of trees and other plants) may be many miles apart within the parrot's habitat. However, parrots make use of their high-speed flying abilities to forage extensively for a range of foods. Most parrots, such as African grays, Amazons and macaws, are largely tree-dwelling and feed in the treetops. But others, such as some cockatoos, some macaws and many

Below: *Parrots are the only birds that use their feet like we use our hands. Most species can hold food like this ring-necked parakeet does to examine it and break it apart before swallowing. The coordination between the eye, foot and beak is a learned, not innate, skill, and it takes a bird some time to be adept at manipulating food in this way.*

Above: *A Timneh gray uses its tongue to test the texture of a grape before deciding if it is sweet enough to eat. Moist fruits are dealt with by lapping up the juice.*

of the smaller species, like cockatiels and budgerigars, are also ground feeders or take food from low-growing grasses and other plants.

The parrot's beak is designed to allow the bird to gain access to (and process) a range of foods. Unique among birds, parrots can use their feet in combination with their beak to feed. The foot is used like a human hand and holds and manipulates small items of food. Parrots tend to favor one foot, just as humans tend to favor one hand. Unlike humans, however, most are left-footed when feeding. Depending on the type of food, parrots have many feeding techniques. With soft fruits, the birds will often just mash up the food in situ, then drink the

The biology of parrots

resulting juices with a rapid lapping action of the tongue. Soft fruits like grapes are usually peeled. A huge range of seeds can be cracked open easily and many hard nuts, which would be impossible for other animals to make use of, can be opened by parrots with only a little more effort. The nut is held in the foot and manipulated to find the weakest spot. Parrots use their tongues as we use our fingers, and the tongue examines the surface of the nut for any weak spots. The point of the upper bill or the chisel-shaped lower bill is then used to stab into this precise point on the nut.

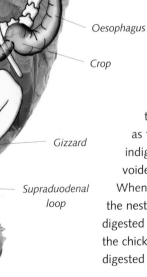

Proventriculus

Oesophagus

Crop

Gizzard

Supraduodenal loop

Duodenum

Cloaca

FOOD CHEWED BEFORE SWALLOWING

These behaviors are not instinctive, and young wild parrots have to spend some time learning how to deal with otherwise inaccessible sources of food if they are to survive. Many other birds that eat seeds, such as ducks and chickens, cannot chew their food before swallowing it, and these birds have to have grit in the gizzard (stomach) to do the chewing for them. But using their powerful bills, parrots chew their food before swallowing it, so most of them do not need to use grit as substitute "teeth" to aid digestion. This prechewing of food again aids in rapid digestion. Initially, the swallowed food is held in the crop, a sacklike part of the gut. From here food is gradually released into the upper stomach (the proventriculus), where proper digestion begins. Next it passes to the gizzard, a muscular part of the stomach where it is further broken down under great pressure from the grinding action of this part of the gut. Further nutrients are extracted as food passes along the intestines, and indigestible items and waste products are voided via the cloaca.

When parrots are feeding their own chicks in the nest, the parent birds regurgitate partially digested food for the chicks from their crop. As the chicks develop, the regurgitated food is less digested and given in a coarser consistency.

Left: *A parrot's digestive tract is quite short. This, combined with the bird's high normal body temperature (about 106°F/41°C), ensures rapid digestion of foods. Most food passes through the bird within a matter of minutes, not hours.*

Living with a parrot

What should you expect? Noise and the beak! Parrots are not generally quiet birds, and adult birds often make a lot more noise than immature birds (birds under 2 years old). When a bird first arrives in its new home it is often quiet for a few days, or even a few weeks, as it settles in. However, it does not usually take long for a bird to get used to its new surroundings, and then it is likely to vocalize at a level normal for its

BE PREPARED FOR NOISE!

While all parrots do make some noise, some species can be particularly loud. Cockatoos and macaws are capable of making sounds that are the loudest of all birds. Sometimes, these birds can be heard well over a mile away when they are emitting their contact or alarm calls. In contrast, African and Timneh gray parrots, pionus parrots and poicephalus parrots (such as the Jardine's, Senegal and Meyer's) are generally less noisy. However, you should always be aware of the potential for a bird to make a considerable amount of noise. Even if you can cope with the noise yourself, please consider your neighbors before acquiring a bird. Disputes between neighbors about noise are quite common, and some parrots can make sounds as loud as any

Left and below: *Some parrots, such as cockatoos (below) and this macaw (left), can be very loud. You should be confident with parrots and not afraid of the odd bite.*

species. Parrots' calls are designed to carry to other birds who may be some distance away, but calls of high volume are usually of a short duration and generally occur early in the morning, and again in the evening. Each session does not usually last more than 30 minutes.

DIY enthusiast. Indeed parrots are often re-homed simply because the owners or their neighbors could not cope with the noise.

If you are nervous of a parrot's beak you should make sure you overcome this anxiety before getting a parrot. If a bird knows that you

Above: *A male eclectus parrot. Unlike many parrots, these birds need a fruit-based diet with little seed.*
Below: *This African gray has chewed the top of a door; this task only takes a few short sessions, while the bird's owner is not looking or is otherwise engaged.*

are afraid of its beak, it is very likely to bite you and may do so repeatedly as it tests your reaction to being bitten. Once this starts to happen, any lack of confidence on your part is likely to stimulate the bird to bite you again, thus reinforcing the behavior. Unless you correct this situation by calmly and confidently training the bird (see section on Training, pages 60–83), you are unlikely to enjoy a trusting relationship with the bird.

THE URGE TO CHEW

Being extremely inquisitive birds, parrots make a lot of use of their beaks. With captive parrots, this means they are likely to be quite destructive and tear apart anything they can. This can include anything made of wood, including your best furniture, door frames and ornaments. While this behavior can, to some extent, be redirected onto appropriate objects (the bird's own toys), most parrots will cause some damage around the home. The larger Amazons, macaws and cockatoos can be very adept at demolishing woodwork. Parrots can be messy birds as well; they will investigate everything, and this often means things get thrown onto the floor as they play with your valuable ornaments. So if you are particularly house-proud, a parrot may not be the best type of pet animal for you.

Expect a long life span

One other parrot characteristic needs to be remembered: most species have a lifespan that is similar to human life expectancy. Unlike other pet animals, parrots, particularly the medium-sized and larger species, are likely to outlive their owners. Lifespan is around 50 to 60 years for birds such as African grays, Amazon parrots, macaws and cockatoos. Even the smaller species, such as Meyer's and Senegal parrots, can live for over 25 years. Many parrots are passed down to the next generation to be cared for. Responsible owners who are no longer in the first flush of youth will need to make provisions for the care of their bird when they are no longer around to look after it.

As active birds, parrots should not be expected simply to stay in their cages or, when out, just to stay on a stand. Activity should be positively encouraged so as to ensure that the bird has a stimulating environment. Many pets, particularly mammals such as guinea pigs, cats and even some dogs, are often cuddled and petted for long periods. However, parrots should not be subjected to such treatment as they can become overstimulated and bond to one person only. This can make them behave aggressively to other members of your family.

Above: *Medium- and larger-sized species, such as this blue and gold macaw, can easily outlive their owners.*

Above: *Parrots, like this Meyer's parrot, need a range of stimulating toys to keep their beaks and brains busy.*

NOT LOW-MAINTENANCE PETS

In order to maintain a good relationship with your bird, you will need to ensure it is trained to accept some basic requests, or commands, from you as explained later in this book. As they are very intelligent birds, parrots usually learn new things very quickly, but they often behave like mischievous children and sometimes get into trouble as a result. It is sensible to recognize that parrots are not low-maintenance pets. Caring for them properly will require that you and your

Living with a parrot

family spend a good deal of time with them every day, and the bird will need to spend many hours each day out of its cage being with you. When parrots do not get the attention they need, they can quickly develop behavioral problems such as nervousness, aggression or feather-plucking, and these can be difficult problems to solve.

Most parrots will test their owner's tolerance from time to time, either with the level of noise, occasional biting, damage to household objects and furniture, and the mess they can make. With these points in mind, there are other less-demanding and less-destructive creatures that might make a better pet for you and your family. Also, if your bird becomes ill, you should be prepared for expensive vet's bills. You should ideally insure your bird to cover the cost of veterinary treatment.

Despite the above caveats, in the right hands parrots can make very rewarding companion animals because of their outgoing, inquisitive natures and their desire to be involved in whatever they see you doing. Many parrot-keepers attest to the depth of the relationship that can develop between a parrot and its carer. This relationship can last for as long as you live.

Above: *The overgrown scales on this Amazon's feet are another sign of aging. Also, an old bird's claws may not wear down and can need filing or cutting at times.*

Keeping parrots should never be dull! Parrots are not passive pets and should not be bought just for their looks or the status they might convey. They are highly intelligent, but sensitive, creatures that can become a real part of your family and that will be with you for many decades. If you are certain that you have the time and dedication needed for these demanding animals, you will find parrots to be very rewarding creatures, but do be aware that taking on one of these birds is a real commitment.

Below: *Older birds, such as this orange-winged Amazon, have poorer feather growth and become slower in their movements when age takes its effect.*

The scaly appearance of the beak is usually quite normal.

Different types of parrots

Although there are over 330 species of parrots, only a few dozen species are regularly kept as companion birds. This section looks at each of these main types. While parrots do have a lot of traits in common with one another, there are important differences between the various types, and it is worth bearing these points in mind when deciding what specie of bird might be suitable for you.

The main groups of parrots that are usually kept as companion birds comprise the following types: Amazons, cockatoos, gray parrots,

Above: *Yellow-naped Amazons. Large Amazons need careful handling as they can easily become overexcited.*
Left: *Red-lored Amazon—quite a popular pet bird.*

macaws, conures, small parrots, parakeets, lovebirds, cockatiels and budgerigars.

AMAZON PARROTS

These are medium-sized to fairly large birds. Most are mainly green in color with patches of red, yellow and blue on their wings, tail and head. Amazons tend to be very outgoing, extroverted birds once they have settled into their new home. They can be a bit like unruly children and need to be with people who are calm and confident with birds. They have powerful beaks and loud voices, though some are much quieter than others, even others of the same species. It is "normal" for adult Amazons to have regular screaming sessions of around 20 minutes each morning and again in

orange-winged Amazon is also popular but less extroverted than the blue-fronted. Care needs to be taken with some adult male Amazons (birds over 3 years old), particularly the larger species as they can be aggressive. This aggression is usually seasonal, starting in the early spring and subsiding after one or two months. Females are less prone to such seasonal aggression. The pionus group includes species such as the red-vented and Maximilian's parrots. These are smaller and have much quieter voices, and they are less excitable than the other Amazon parrots and can make very good pets. These birds do not usually copy human speech. Hawk-headed parrots are known to be particularly aggressive and are not recommended as pet birds.

Above: *A bronze-winged pionus parrot. Pionus parrots are not as loud as most other types of parrot.*
Right: *The orange-winged Amazon is probably the most common Amazon kept as a pet bird.*
Far right: *A blue-fronted Amazon.*

the evening, and they can have very loud voices. Most Amazons kept as companion birds learn to talk and, unlike gray parrots, will often talk in the company of strangers.

Blue-fronted Amazons are fairly typical of the larger Amazons and are very popular as companion birds, being lively characters. The similarly colored but slightly smaller

Cockatoos, African grays & Timneh grays

COCKATOOS

Most cockatoos are as big as, or larger than, the Amazons. They are extremely sensitive and nervous birds while being very intelligent. Most are mainly white in color with infusions of yellow or pink on the wings and tail. Unlike other parrots, cockatoos have erectile crests that can be raised and lowered at will. Species such as the Moluccan cockatoo and sulfur-crested cockatoo are kept as pet birds, with other types, such as the Goffin's and little corella, less commonly seen as pets.

Cockatoos tend to have very loud voices and, as adults, indulge in regular screaming periods in the morning and again in the evening. Many people buy these birds because they look cute and cuddly as youngsters. However, as with any creature, when they mature their behavior changes. These birds often seem to find captivity very frustrating, and they are inclined to develop serious behavioral problems as young adults, when 2 to 4 years old. Some become very nervous, others become aggressive and very loud. As adults, the larger species can inflict very serious and painful bites if you have not trained the bird to accept the usual commands from you.

The pair bond in cockatoos is extremely strong, perhaps stronger than in any other parrotlike bird. Due to this characteristic, cockatoos commonly end up being one-person birds as adults, demanding constant attention from one particular person only. Sadly, some people who have bought an appealing young bird end up selling it a few months or a few years later because they are not able to cope with such a demanding bird, and cockatoos often end up in rescue centers. Many cockatoos, particularly those that have been hand-reared, are also prone to feather plucking as they leave their juvenile stage and become adults. Although these birds look extremely appealing, they are usually too difficult for most people to care for properly, and they are not recommended as pet birds. The smaller galah, however, is the exception here. This bird is much more easygoing, and most adapt well to life as a pet bird.

Above left: *Umbrella cockatoo—a demanding pet bird.*
Above right: *Major Mitchell's cockatoo—rare in captivity.*
Top center: *The galah—a small but extrovert cockatoo.*

Different types of parrots

AFRICAN AND TIMNEH GRAYS

These are the most commonly kept medium- to large-sized pet parrots. There are two types of gray parrots, the Timneh gray and the African, or Congo, gray. These birds had been thought to be one species with minor differences between them. However, there is increasing evidence that they are two separate species. The Timneh is about two-thirds the size of the African gray, with darker gray, almost black, plumage. Timnehs always have a pale horn-colored area on the upper bill, and their tail is dark red or maroon, never bright red as in African grays.

Gray parrots tend to be very wary of any new situation, and they are generally rather nervous and very sensitive birds. That said, Timnehs do seem to have more confidence than African grays. These birds are renowned for their abilities to mimic a wide range of sounds, including human speech, and the quality of their voices is among the best found in birds. However, grays are often reluctant to talk in the presence of strangers. While most grays kept as pet birds do learn to talk, some birds never copy human speech. Hand-reared gray parrots are very prone to feather plucking, but parent-reared birds, though less tame initially, tend to be at less risk of developing behavioral problems.

Gray parrots are extremely intelligent birds, and much scientific work has been carried out in the U.S. on their abilities to learn and use human language in its proper context (not merely for mimicry). When it comes to their abilities to label and describe a range of objects shown to them, grays show a level of intelligence similar to a

Above right: *African gray—the most popular pet parrot.*
Above left: *The Timneh gray is a smaller relative of the African gray and has darker plumage.*

human toddler. In the hands of a knowledgeable keeper, these parrots can do well as companion birds. While they can be loud on occasion they rarely become a noise nuisance. Gray parrots are best suited to a fairly quiet home where they will feel more at ease with people. They need to be with people who are calm and confident in their behavior, and they may not do very well in a household with young children or dogs.

Macaws & conures

MACAWS

While the largest parrots are macaws, there are several "mini macaws" as well. The smaller macaws, such as the Hahn's and yellow-collared, can make good pets, though they can be noisy on occasion. Their character is similar to the Amazon parrots (see pages 26–27). They are active, outgoing, inquisitive birds, and they are often mischievous in their antics. Some birds do learn to talk and they can be quite chatty.

Due to their sheer size, the larger macaws, such as the blue and gold, the scarlet and the green-winged, have specialist

Right: *Blue and gold macaw. Because of their large size and very loud calls, most people do not have the capabilities to keep such a bird.*

needs that most people would find very difficult to provide. These birds have a wingspan of around 5 feet (1.5 m). They can be very loud and their powerful beaks can easily demolish furniture, doors, plasterwork and any woodwork, sometimes within a few minutes.

Right: *The green-winged macaw is the largest "common" macaw. Their needs cannot really be met in the ordinary home.*

Macaws do not do very well in cages, even the large ones intended for them, and overuse of a cage can result in them developing behavioral problems.

When kept as companion birds, they need a large indoor aviary rather than a cage, and this should be big enough for them to fly in. They should also have access to a further outdoor flight as well, so they can exercise and keep fit. Some people are intimidated by the sheer size of the birds, and their huge bill and a threat display

Right: *The scarlet macaw is now a rare bird in the wild.*

Different types of parrots

from a macaw can certainly be very alarming. However, despite the large bill, which is capable of easily crushing Brazil nuts, macaws are usually gentle but playful birds. The large macaws are not really suitable for a home with small children, and they can be aggressive toward dogs and cats. Caring for these birds requires facilities that are not available to most people, so take great care when thinking of acquiring one.

Below: *Golden-capped conure. A very lively bird, but can be noisy.*

Above: *Sun conures are popular as pets, but they are very loud birds and can be aggressive as adults.*

CONURES

All conures originate from South America. Generally, conures are very active, fairly small birds that display a degree of confidence not found in many other parrots. Unlike other parrots, conures regularly use their long tails as a prop when climbing around. Consequently they do not use their beak as much as other parrots when climbing. Despite their small size, many, such as the bright orange and yellow sun conure, the Patagonian and blue-crowned conures have loud piercing voices as adult birds. Their outgoing and busy nature make them very entertaining birds interested in everything going on around them. Some conures do learn to talk, but they tend to have small, squeaky voices when using human speech. The smaller species, such as the green-cheeked and maroon-bellied, make better pet birds and are not as loud as some other species.

Conures appreciate being given a roosting box to sleep in at nighttime, and all species should be offered a box of suitable size in their cage, which they will readily take to. Conures are sometimes described as being "nippy" birds and prone to bite readily. This usually happens because they can become overexcited quite easily, so care needs to be exercised to avoid this.

Parakeets & other small parrots

PARAKEETS

The term "parakeet" tends to be very loosely used to cover a wide range of smaller parrotlike birds (apart from conures) that have long tails. Most species come from Australasia or Asia and are mainly very active, leaf-green-colored birds. Kakarikis are popular as pet birds and are around the same size as a budgerigar. These birds are ground-feeders and spend a lot of time rummaging around on the floor of their cage or aviary. Rosellas, which are twice the size of the budgerigar, are also sometimes kept as companion birds indoors, though generally they are best kept with others of their own kind in an

Above left: *A ring-necked parakeet. This is the normal color of the bird as seen in the wild.*
Above right: *Rosellas are usually kept in aviaries.*

aviary. There are many species of small "grass parakeets," such as Bourke's parakeet and the turquoise parakeet, which are active, colorful birds. Unlike most parrots, they are not noisy birds at all.

As parakeets are highly social creatures, normally living in large flocks, they are not usually kept as lone pet birds in cages but more often as aviary birds outdoors. They do not usually bond to their human carer as other parrots do and tend to be self-reliant, indeed very independent, birds. However, some respond quite well to basic training and can make good pet birds. Parakeets rarely mimic human speech. While most are not noisy birds, the ring-necked parakeet does have a very loud voice. This species escaped many years ago in southern Britain and many thousands now breed freely in the wild in the U.K.

Above: *Ring-necked parakeets are usually kept as an aviary bird, but sometimes as a pet indoors. These birds are bred in a range of different color mutations.*

Different types of parrots

PARROTLETS

These are the smallest of all parrots, and they are really very tiny birds, being about the size of a sparrow. These mainly green parrots are becoming more popular as pet birds as they are perceived to be easy birds to keep in cages. However, they too need plenty of time out of their cages to fly around. They do bond to humans (more so than lovebirds tend to, see below) so can be quite demanding of time. Their voices can be loud at times, but they are not generally noisy birds.

Above: *These Mexican parrolets are among the smallest parrots.*

POICEPHALUS PARROTS AND CAIQUES

These smaller- to medium-sized parrots are very underrated as pets. Most are mainly green birds with patches of yellow and brown on the body and wings. This group, which includes the Senegal parrot, Meyer's parrot, Jardine's parrot and the caiques, can become very good pet

birds. They are much more active and outgoing than gray parrots and certainly more confident in their behavior. They are very strong-willed birds, often described as feisty with a determined nature. While many parrots regard most new situations or objects, including new toys, with suspicion, these birds have a quite different attitude. Invariably, they are quite fearless and keen to investigate anything new.

They are also very demanding of attention and affection, frequently asking for their heads to be scratched. While their voices can be loud, this is rarely a problem. These birds sometimes learn to speak a few words and are good at mimicking many sounds, though they are not renowned for their talking abilities. However, they more than make up for this with their extrovert, clowning nature. Poicephalus parrots and caiques cope much better than almost all other species at living with people as companion birds.

Above right: *The Meyer's parrot has the determination of the caique; they are often fearless birds with a big ego.*
Left: *A black-headed caique. This is a smaller, very active, outgoing parrot with a determined nature.*

Eclectus, lovebirds, cockatiels & budgies

ECLECTUS PARROTS

These are medium-sized to fairly large parrots, quite different from other parrotlike birds. The males and females have such different plumage that at one time they were thought to be separate species. The males are mainly a bright leaf-green with red and blue patches on their flanks and wings. But the females are bright red with patches of purple or blue on their flanks and wings. Unlike other parrots, the nostrils of this bird are hidden in a growth of fine feathers above the upper bill. The body feathers of eclectus parrots are extremely fine and almost hairlike. The birds' natural habitat is tropical rain forest, where they eat a diet of fruits, flowers, buds and some seeds. The birds are very beautiful and are often bought merely for their color. However, they do not usually adapt well to being kept as indoor companion birds and can be both very noisy and aggressive as adults. They are also prone to self-plucking behaviors.

Above: *Fischer's lovebirds are popular aviary birds and are sometimes kept as pets indoors.*
Below left: *A female red-sided eclectus*
Below far left: *A male red-sided eclectus.*

LOVEBIRDS

These small, short-tailed parrots originate from Africa. They are very active birds but are best kept as pairs rather than as single pet birds. While some are kept singly as pets, they do not usually bond to humans in the way most other parrots do. They have shrill voices and can make calls at a volume out of all proportion to their size. They do not copy human speech. In general these birds are best kept as aviary birds rather than companion pets.

Different types of parrots

COCKATIELS AND BUDGIES

These are the most common smaller parrotlike pet birds, and they both come from Australia. Both species are now semi-domesticated and all birds offered for sale are bred in captivity. The qualities of the budgerigar are well known. This is not a difficult bird to keep, but if kept on its own the bird needs a lot of time with its keeper, including much time out of its cage each day to fly. Some budgies learn to talk very well, being capable of learning many words and phrases, though they have a small, squeaky voice. Budgies are certainly active, busy birds and on the go for most of the day. The natural color of the budgerigar is bright green below with a fine scalelike pattern of black and white markings above. However, there is a huge range of color types of budgerigar that have been derived through selective breeding in captivity over many generations.

Cockatiels are larger and can also make good pet birds; these too come in a range of color mutations, though the natural color

is gray with white on the wings and yellow-orange patches on the head. Cockatiels can learn to talk, but they can also have loud, harsh voices when using their contact calls. Again these are very active birds that tend to keep themselves busy. As with other parrots, both cockatiels and budgies can be taught to obey some requests, or commands, from their carer, as described later.

Left: *The blue cere (nostrils) show this to be a male budgie.*
Below: *Cockatiels are lively and inquisitive birds as pets.*

Acquiring a parrot

Very tame cuddly parrots are often offered for sale at breeders' premises, in pet stores and at some garden centers. These very young birds are also advertised for sale in bird-keeping magazines. However, like all babies, these birds soon grow up. This process varies with the species, but generally smaller types mature quicker than the larger species. So, it takes only 18 months for a conure or poicephalus parrot to mature fully, but up to 4 years for Amazons, gray parrots, macaws and cockatoos. It is important to bear in mind that a parrot's adult behavior will almost certainly be utterly different from its juvenile behavior.

Above: *Baby African grays, at about 9 weeks of age. They are often offered for sale when they are only 13 weeks old, which is far too young for them to be sold.*

AGE-RELATED BEHAVIORS

The reason why a baby parrot behaves differently to an adult is much the same as why any baby animal behaves in this way. Most immature creatures adopt very submissive behaviors that encourage others to treat them gently. This

Right: *A baby Major Mitchell's cockatoo. This is a beautiful species, but it is not easy to keep as a pet bird.*

behavioral appeasement trait is seen in many animals, such as puppies and kittens, and is an instinctive survival technique. In the pet store or breeder's premises, these birds can seem very appealing and can be handled very easily. However, as the bird matures, its needs change, and so naturally does its behavior. This is to be expected. An adult, sexually mature parrot has a very different set of urges to one that is only 6 months old! So be well aware of this when you see immature parrots for sale.

Most parrots that are produced for the pet trade (as opposed to aviary birds or birds to be used for breeding) are raised by being hand-fed. Hand-rearing is usually carried out by the breeder removing the eggs from the parent birds and using an incubator to hatch them. Once the chicks have hatched out, they are then fed by hand. This process takes from four to 16 weeks, with the larger species taking the longer period. In bigger commercial breeding units some chicks are force-fed by crude methods, and these birds may have no interactions with any other birds. Since these birds have not been raised by their own parents and may not even have had the company of any other parrots, they tend to become obsessed with humans, and this results in the so-called "imprinting" behaviors. Here, as soon as the birds are fledged and are at the age where they would naturally leave the nest, they only want to be with people and not other parrots.

THE EFFECTS OF HAND-REARING

Parrots raised in this artificial way, being deprived of normal parental interactions, may develop serious behavioral problems, but these usually only manifest themselves upon maturity at around 2 to 4 years old. Typically, these problems can include over-bonding to one person and showing aggression to others due to "jealousy." If you decide to acquire an immature bird, it is best if you can obtain one that has been parent-reared,

Below left and right: *How birds are raised from hatching can affect their behavior for the rest of their lives. Hand-reared birds, though endearing at first, can be difficult to live with when they grow older.*

Above: *Quaker parakeets, about the size of a cockatiel, can make good pet birds.*

or at least part-parent-reared, rather than one hand-reared from the day it hatched. Parrots that have been raised mainly by their own natural parents are unlikely to develop obsessive behaviors, such as repetitive screaming, and as adults are more likely to behave like "normal" birds, possessed of a degree of self-confidence and independence that is not usually seen in hand-reared birds.

Buying baby birds

Baby birds may still sometimes be offered for sale at itinerant "pet fairs" — one-day events where pets are often sold cheaper than those in pet stores or breeder's premises. Conditions for the birds at these events are often poor and receipts and guarantees are not normally given

Above: *Avoid buying birds in conditions such as these budgies are enduring in an overcrowded cage at a pet fair; they could be carrying diseases.*

for any bird purchased. Birds on sale may be diseased and you may be sold a bird on false information, so it is best to avoid buying any birds at such places. Bona fide breeders and pet stores will hold a proper license that regulates how they trade in their birds. Birds from these establishments will almost certainly cost more than those from other outlets, but it is worth paying a bit extra to make sure you get a healthy bird. Most good-quality pet stores and breeders will ensure you have a receipt and some form of guarantee with any bird you buy, plus detailed information on how to care for it. If you are not offered this service, make sure to ask for these

things. Responsible pet stores and breeders should also be able to offer you better advice on how to care for your bird.

DON'T BUY TOO SOON

It is not recommended that you buy a bird so young bird that it is not fully weaned and feeding itself independently of its parents or hand-rearer. A young bird should be fully able to feed itself and have been doing so for several weeks before it is offered for sale. It is still common for birds such as grays and Amazons to be sold at around 13 weeks old, with the seller claiming they are fully weaned. Unless you already have considerable experience of hand-feeding baby birds, you should not take on a bird that cannot feed itself properly. In the wild, most young parrots stay with their parents not merely for a few weeks, but for many months or even a year or more. During this time they learn, by trial and error, how to eat a large range of different foods and how to behave appropriately and interact with other parrots. If you do decide to get a young bird, it is best to make sure it is several months old before you take it on. You can of course offer to put a deposit down on a

Left to far right: *Parrots hatch as naked and helpless babies. The age at which they fledge (leave the nest) varies and tends to take several months for larger species, but only several weeks for smaller birds.*

Acquiring a parrot

Above left and right: *Development of the baby birds is quite slow in larger species, like this blue and gold macaw. A baby macaw may not leave the nest until it is 3 months old. Even then, it is reliant on its parents for many months after it leaves the nest.*

particular bird and only collect it when you are happy that it is old enough.

Some parrot experts may suggest that you do not spend too much time with an immature bird when you first obtain it, so that it can get used to being on its own for longer periods. This is very poor advice and can cause serious behavioral problems in young birds. One would never leave a human toddler on its own for hours so that it got used to it. Young birds, like any young animal, have different needs and abilities than those they will have as adults. Therefore, it is vital that an immature bird is never without company for most of the daytime. Only when the bird is older might it be possible to leave it on its own for a longer period; even then, such periods alone run the risk of causing behavioral problems if they are too frequent. The bird should be introduced very carefully and gradually to this process only when it is old enough to cope with it.

Getting an older bird

Of course, you do not have to acquire a young bird—you may wish to opt for an older one. There is already an excess of parrots being produced for the pet trade, while plenty of

Below: *If a bird on sale in a pet store like this is offered as "tame," make sure that this is the case before buying it and ask to see it being handled as proof.*

older parrots are frequently advertised in bird-keeping magazines. Also, there are some advantages to getting an older bird. Parrots are very intelligent and (in the right hands) very adaptable birds, and an older bird can certainly be a better option. Once a bird is mature, its true character will

be revealed and, unlike immature birds, a mature bird's character will not change greatly over the coming years. Provided you train the bird (see pages 60–83) many older birds make very good companion animals.

TRY ADOPTING A BIRD

From time to time some parrot rescue centers will foster birds out. No purchase is made, but you can usually keep, but not actually own, a fostered bird indefinitely so long as you agree to the conditions that are stipulated by the rescue center in their adoption scheme. In effect, these adoptions are similar to the schemes run by shelters for cats and dogs in need of good homes.

When acquiring an older bird, it is important to find out as much as you can about the bird's history from the present owner, and to ask them why they are selling the bird at this point. Many will have genuine reasons for having to part with the bird, and parrots often outlive their first or even second owners. But make sure that you see the current

Above: *It usually takes longer to get to know an older bird really well, and they may not show the submissive behaviors commonly seen in immature parrots.*

Acquiring a parrot

relevant. However, to prevent any behavioral problems from setting in, it is best to start training your bird to accept some commands from almost as soon as you get it. Don't wait for the bird to settle in for several weeks; instead, start the training within a few days of getting it. By starting with the basic training quite quickly, you have a much better chance of preventing problems in the first place. Birds that are not trained may become either nervous or aggressive and will not know how to relate to you and other members of your family. Nervous, more introverted or less confident birds, such as some cockatoos and gray parrots, may become withdrawn and fearful, but careful training can prevent this.

Above: *Larger species, like this scarlet macaw, can live for over 50 years and often outlive their owners. It's well worth considering an older bird, even though they may take some time to adjust to you as the new owner.*

owner handling the bird so that you know that it is tame. Ask about the bird's likes and dislikes and how it has been kept. Some older birds may display behavioral problems, such as self-plucking, or they may be very noisy. However, with sympathetic care these problems can often be reduced, if not completely cured, and you may well be able to take better care of the bird if its current owners are not able to give it the care it deserves.

STARTING TO TRAIN YOUR BIRD

Most breeders and pet stores do not train their birds to accept any commands from people, so you will have to do the training yourself. Birds can learn new skills at any age so, from the training point of view, the age of the bird is not

Above: *Don't delay the training of your bird. In most cases you should be able to start this within a few days of acquiring the bird, which will usually be as interested in trying to get to know you as you are in it.*

Checking the condition of the bird

Birds offered for sale should be in good condition, but it is important to be aware of signs that all may not be well before you part with your money.

A healthy bird will be bright and alert, well aware and interested in things going on around it. The eyes should be wide open and bright, not sunken in, dull or with the eyelids half closed. There should be no discharge from the nostrils, which should be unobstructed and clean. The underside of the bird should also be clean, with no traces of droppings on the bird's feathers.

Left: *When seen in good light, a healthy parrot's feathers have a slight "bloom" to them, being almost glossy.*

The general condition of the bird's feathers tells much about its well being. Feathers should not be frayed or damaged but be in good condition, usually with a certain "bloom" on them, which gives a semigloss effect in good light. When birds are caged, feather abrasion is common on the leading edges of the main flight feathers and on the tail. Slight damage here is not a particular concern, but serious abrasions could indicate self-plucking. Self-plucking often also starts with the bird damaging the feathers around its chest

Above: *This female eclectus is in poor feather condition. Note the frayed tail and wing feathers and clipped wing.*

or on the "shoulders" or the bend of the wings. Normally, the body feathers should not be fluffed up but smoothed down, though not with an excessive tightness. A bird with fluffed-up feathers, particularly one that is largely inactive, is very likely to be·unwell.

FURTHER SIGNS TO CHECK

When resting, healthy birds usually stand on one foot and tuck the other one up under their belly. Resting birds that stand on

Left: *This African gray has a severe wing-clip to his left wing and could suffer a serious injury if he tried to fly.*

Acquiring a parrot

both feet may be having difficulty balancing and this, too, can be a sign of illness. Check also for any deformities. The feet should grip the perch squarely. Birds with deformed feet may have been subjected to vitamin and mineral deficiencies during their first few weeks of life. Check to see that the bird has all of its claws. All parrots have four toes, but if the bird has been fighting with another bird some of its toes or claws may be damaged or missing.

When buying any immature bird, you should check thoroughly to see if it has been wing-clipped. For the sake of a young bird's health and welfare it should not be clipped; indeed, at this stage of its development it should be encouraged to take proper exercise each day by being able to fly. If you do see a young bird that you would like to have but that has been clipped, you could ask the owner to have its wings repaired before you buy it. This can be done by a specialist avian vet. Alternatively, you could have this done when you acquire the bird. For details of how this is performed, see the section on imping on pages 110–111. When getting an older bird that has been clipped, check to see that the clipping is not so severe that it would cause the bird to

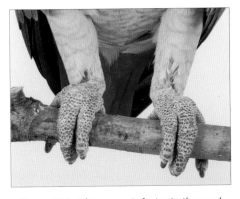

Above: *This African gray's feet grip the perch squarely and evenly.*

lose its balance if it tried to fly. Any bird that has been clipped should only have a light clip to both wings; this allows it to land without crashing and injuring itself. Birds clipped on one wing only are very prone to serious accidents. Again, any improper clipping can be repaired as above.

Below: *To check the condition of the wings, count the main outer flight feathers; there should be 9 or 10 of these primaries, as can be seen on this Meyer's parrot.*

Hold the wing at the wrist joint when extending it.

Taking your bird home

Care needs to be exercised when taking a bird to a new location. Parrots are well aware of everything going on around them, and you must try to minimize stress for the bird when taking it home. Tame birds can usually be placed directly into a small traveling cage. Birds that are not tame will need to be carefully caught in a towel, then placed into the traveling cage as they are released from the towel. Birds will enter an all-wire traveling cage more readily than one with a dark, boxlike construction. However, during actual transit birds will remain much calmer if their vision is restricted. With this in mind, cover the all-wire cage with a cloth or towel after the bird has been placed inside it. This cage should have a single low perch fitted securely and located centrally near the base. For journeys of more than two hours, food—particularly wet foods such as

Left: Clear plastic carriers are fine, but they should be well ventilated and partially covered with a cloth during transit.

grapes or pieces of apple— should be provided.

PREPARE THE CAGE IN ADVANCE

The bird's new home cage should be set up before the bird arrives with its usual food (and water) already placed in it. The cage should be situated with its back against a wall so that the bird has a solid surface behind it; this will ensure that the bird feels more secure. The top perch in the cage should be at, or just below, your eye level. If this perch is too low, the bird may feel excessively vulnerable.

After leaving the pet store or breeder's premises, the bird suddenly has to cope with an avalanche of changes. It will meet new people, have a new cage and many of the sights and

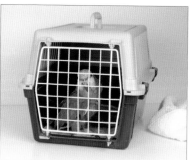

Above left and center: *A traveling cage should have solid sides to restrict the bird's vision and a perch fitted just above the floor. Use a towel to help handling.*

Above right: *Birds can be trained to walk into a carrier, and they will do so more readily with an all-wire type. This should be covered with a cloth when in transit.*

Left: *Ensure the top perch is not too low in the cage —nor should the food bowls be positioned too low down.*

sounds it hears in your home will be unfamiliar. These experiences can cause the bird to seem very wary for a while, so it is important to make any other changes gradually so as not to upset the bird. At this stage don't change the bird's food; keep it on the same diet for the time being. And don't introduce new toys until a day or two after it has been with you. Also, don't interact with the bird continuously on the first day you have it. By keeping things calm, the bird should settle in well and start to accept all the new things around it.

TAKE CARE WITH FLYING BIRDS

If you have acquired a young bird it may be clumsy when trying to fly but this is quite normal. At this stage, young birds are like small children learning to walk instead of crawl. So the bird may sometimes crash-land or misjudge distances and bump into things. On seeing this, some people clip their bird's wings in the mistaken (and actually dangerous) belief that this will help. However, this will only make matters worse, particularly for a young bird. Once clipped, the bird will still try to fly, since at this age parrots have a strong urge to learn to fly as part of their normal survival strategy. But if clipped the bird will have even

less control and less confidence than normal, which will confuse it. Indeed, such wing-clipping of young birds can result in serious problems quite quickly. So at this stage, just allow the bird to develop its flying skills as best it can.

Do make sure, of course, to prevent collisions with windows and mirrors. Mirrors can usually be removed and windows should be at least partially covered up while your bird is out of its cage. Also, to minimize flying accidents for a young bird, you'll need to introduce the bird carefully to the room(s) to which it will have access. To do this, undertake several sessions of asking the bird to step from your hand down onto (and off) safe places, such as the top of its cage or stand or the back of a chair, etc. (see the section on training on pages 66–69 for details of how to do this). Once introduced to the best perching places, when your bird does fly it will tend to return to these when landing, rather than crash-landing elsewhere.

Left: *Always remain calm and confident with new or nervous birds, so as not to upset them in their new home.*

Understanding behavior

INSTINCTIVE BEHAVIORS

The question why any creature, including ourselves and other intelligent creatures such as parrots, behave in the way they do is a complex subject. And compared to other subjects, the scientific study of behavior is a fairly new field. Some behaviors that we see in animals are largely innate; that is, they are carried out instinctively. We have little or no control over these behaviors: there are three types of them—reflex behaviors, fixed action patterns and innate behavioral tendencies.

Reflex behaviors include such things as our blinking reflex and our avoidance of hot surfaces by withdrawing our hand rapidly. These actions are not under our conscious control and occur due to an external

Both above: *A parrot's eye will close briefly when anything approaches its face suddenly or touches it near the eyes. This Meyer's parrot is caught as it blinks momentarily.*

stimulus. Parrots have many reflex actions. They will blink just as we do when something approaches their eyes very closely, and they will turn to face a sudden sound or action. Baby parrots have a food-begging behavior that is elicited by the presence of one or both parents on returning to the nest.

Fixed action patterns are more complex behaviors. In parrots they include things such as the way they stretch their limbs. All parrots stretch either their left leg and wing together, or the right leg and wing together as they stand on their other leg. Also, parrots always

Left: *Parrots feed their mates and babies by regurgitating partially digested food from the crop. When a baby bird wants to be fed, it begs by touching its mother's beak when she returns to the nest.*

glide with their wing tips help down, lower than their back; conversely, pigeons glide with their wing tips help up in a V formation. The bird has little control over these actions; they are hard-wired to perform them as part of their genetic makeup and no real learning is involved.

Innate behavioral traits are also instinctive behaviors but are more complex still. They can be used to describe a bird's general character. Budgerigars tend to be very busy and inquisitive birds, and eclectus parrots tend to be rather sedentary, even lazy by comparison. Unlike the other two types of behavior, these behaviors can have a learned component and be modified by things the bird experiences throughout its life. The origins of these three types of behavior lie in the bird's genes. These behaviors have evolved for the same reasons as all other evolved conditions: they increase each bird's chances of survival in its habitat, so every behavior has a clear purpose or function.

Below left and right: *These pictures allow comparison of the fixed action patterns in a gliding pigeon compared with a gliding macaw. The pigeon's wings are always held up; the macaw's are held down.*

LEARNED BEHAVIORS

In the 1890s the first scientific experiments were carried out on animal behavior, and they were able to confirm that animals did not simply rely on a repertoire of instinctive behaviors but could easily learn many new behaviors. They showed that these learned behaviors were performed because the animal was aware that desirable consequences would result from the behavior. So the first principles of behaviorism came to be understood: that behavior is a function of its own consequences.

Later, this theme was developed by the Russian physiologist Ivan Pavlov, who conditioned a dog to salivate (anticipate food) on hearing a bell. This conditioned, learned reflex (the sound of the bell allied to the provision of food) showed that animals could easily learn new things. Modern behavioral work was further carried out by B.F. Skinner in the 1930s. He refined Pavlov's work placing more emphasis on the animals' abilities to learn new things. Indeed, Skinner is often seen as the founder of applied behavior analysis, which can be defined as the science of behavior change.

Applied behavior analysis

While a wide range of methods are promoted and claim to show how to change a bird's behavior or tame it or solve various behavioral problems, the only scientific method of behavior change is applied behavior analysis (ABA). Just as the medical care of birds is based on sound scientific principles of veterinary medicine, ABA puts the question of behavior on a similar scientific grounding. ABA concentrates simply on observable behaviors and how these can either be increased, decreased or even eliminated. While parrots certainly have their own thoughts and feelings, ABA does not delve into such things, since thoughts and feelings cannot be seen or measured in terms of their frequency or intensity. Instead, ABA works by careful observation of what we actually *see* the bird doing and the frequency of the behaviors.

Below: *This African gray's preening actions are innate behaviors.*

Above: *This Timneh gray enjoys a head scratch, which can be a useful means of rewarding a bird for good behaviors.*

The instinctive behaviors mentioned earlier cannot be controlled by the bird, and you should not attempt to try to change such behaviors. Rather, the behaviors we are looking at are all "voluntary" behaviors; behaviors that the bird can control and has learned and decided to perform. These may be desirable behaviors, like a bird flying to you because it likes being with you, or undesirable behaviors, such as a bird that bites your hand or refuses to step up onto your hand. All these behaviors have

Understanding behavior

a cause, and the bird gets some desirable consequences by performing each behavior, so we know that these behaviors have a flexibility not seen in innate behaviors. The provision of a desirable consequence (a reward) immediately following a behavior will tend to reinforce such behavior, which simply means it is more likely to be repeated. By appreciating

Below: *A food sampling selection to determine a favorite item. Offer your bird several items all together like this to see which it goes for first.*

Sunflower seed   Almond   Cashew

Peanut   Walnut   Grape

FIND THE FAVORITE

Food rewards can be used, but some types of food are far more desirable to a parrot than others, so if you are going to use a food reward, you'll need to determine what your particular bird's favorite item is. Generally high-fat foods or very sweet foods are most favored by parrots. When determining the favorite food, often the size of the item is of more interest to the bird than the nature of the food itself, so you need to take this into account and offer similar-sized portions of some known favorite items. You could try the following: half a grape, an almond, a similar-sized piece of bread and peanut butter, or bread and margarine, a peanut, half a walnut, etc. Offer these all at the same time

this, we are on the way to being able to ask our birds to perform certain behaviors provided we can give them a suitable reward to reinforce that behavior. The reward has to be something *the bird* already really likes. It is much the same as rewarding a person for doing some work. If the reward is of sufficient value (if your pay is high enough), you are far more likely to do the task asked of you.

to your bird and see which it takes first and actually eats. Repeat this test four or five times during the day and keep a note of which items it selects first. You'll soon see that it has a preference for one or two particular items, and these are the ones that you can then use as rewards during your training sessions. Withdraw these foods from your bird's food bowls on days when you will be training him.

The A-B-Cs of behavior

When using applied behavior analysis methods to understand specific behaviors, it helps to break down the sequence of events involved into the observable A-B-Cs of behavior. These are:

The **antecedents** (the events immediately prior to the behavior).

The precise **behavior** itself.

The **consequences** for the bird immediately following the behavior.

Here's an example of the A-B-Cs in a Timneh gray parrot that is known to bite on some occasions when being asked to step onto its carer's hand from within the cage. The bird's carer opens the cage door, asks the bird to "step up" onto his hand, but sometimes the bird's feathers are held down tightly, its eye is wide and staring, and it lunges at the carer and bites his hand. Then he removes his bitten hand, closes the cage door and walks away. Divided into the A-B-C terms, this is the sequence:

A Bird's carer opens the cage door and offers his hand as a perch saying "step up."

B Bird holds its body feathers down tightly, and its eyes are wide open and staring as it lunges forward and bites the hand.

C The carer removes his bitten hand, closes the cage door and goes away.

WATCH YOUR BIRD'S BODY LANGUAGE

Here we have a behavior in which we can deduce that the bird sometimes wants the owner to go away (its staring eyes and feathers held down tightly). The owner refuses to do so, the bird bites him, and he *does* then go away. Many people say that a bird will bite without warning.

A *This bird does not wish to come out of its cage at this moment but approaches the owner's hand and...*

B *...bites him, since the owner has not been able to read the bird's body language correctly.*

C *So the owner closes the cage door, walks away and leaves the bird alone for a while.*

Understanding behavior

However, in most cases birds do give a clear indication of their intention to bite. The key thing is to watch your bird's body language very carefully all the time you are interacting with it. Birds' actions and reactions are often very quick and (to humans) very brief—it's as though the bird can communicate the equivalent of a long sentence in the blink of an eye (or the brief raising or lowering of some feathers). Birds certainly seem to live at a much faster rate than humans, so unless you are very attentive, you may miss clear warning signs from the bird.

ALTERING A BEHAVIOR

Following the principles of applied behavior analysis, to change this biting behavior the bird's carer will need to change the antecedents or the consequences of that behavior. The vital part of this change requires the bird's carer to give the bird a reward that he knows the bird already really likes. Knowing that this particular bird's favorite food is grapes, he will give it a grape, but only if and when it steps onto the hand. So, the new A-B-C scenario will look like this:

A The bird's carer opens the cage door and greets the bird, making eye contact and waiting for some indication that it is in a receptive mood (bird calls or raises its head feathers slightly). The carer then uses a new phrase to ask the bird to step up by saying "on here" as he offers his hand.
B The bird steps up.
C He rewards the bird with something he knows the bird really likes; he gives it a grape and returns it to a perch so it can eat it.
The bird is also given verbal praise to associate this response with the food reward.

A *A new approach: the cage door is opened and the bird shown a reward. The bird is more relaxed.*

B *The bird agrees to the request of "on here" and steps up onto the owner's outstretched hand.*

C *The bird then gets his reward of a small food treat, such as a grape, and lots of verbal praise.*

Reinforcement of a behavior

When a behavior continues to occur, it is said to be *reinforced*. In the replacement A-B-C example described on the previous page, the bird was given a favorite food treat as a reward for stepping onto the carer's hand. If this result of stepping up is repeated on subsequent requests from the carer and the bird steps up and ceases to bite, then the desired behavior is being reinforced. But there are two types of reinforcement that result in a behavior continuing: *positive* reinforcement and *negative* reinforcement. Positive reinforcement refers to a situation in which the bird gets something it desires (a reward). Here the actual reward is determined by the bird. With some birds the reward may be a favorite food treat, but another bird might be more strongly motivated by being offered a favorite toy, or by having its head gently scratched. In learning a new behavior, the provision of some reward is vital.

Negative reinforcement occurs when an animal performs a behavior so as to avoid some unpleasant outcome. A horse rider might persuade a horse to go faster by using spurs on the animal's flanks. The horse goes faster simply because it knows that by doing so the rider will ease off the spurs and the discomfort will cease. While negative reinforcement works in the sense that the animal performs the desired behavior, it only does so by causing the animal some discomfort, or even pain. Negative reinforcement should never be used with parrots since pain or discomfort may cause the bird to fear its trainer intensely. This is precisely the opposite of the trusting relationship that one should try to establish with any parrot.

Above: *This Meyer's parrot loves having its head gently scratched, and this can be used as a very effective reward during training sessions.*

CLICKER TRAINING

This is commonly used in training dogs, and sometimes parrots, as an aid to positive reinforcement, and it can be very effective. The trainer uses a small hand-held device that makes a clicking sound when pressed. The

Understanding behavior

Above: *This African gray prefers a food reward to a head scratch so, for this bird, food is a more effective reward at this stage of the training program.*

you and understood by the bird (they learn very quickly), training is not at all difficult to do.

To return to the example of retraining a bird that bites, if, on being offered the hand while giving the new "on here" command and new reward, the bird does show signs that it is about to bite, then the owner should simply withdraw his hand, walk away, close the cage door and leave the bird alone. A further attempt can be tried later.

Below: *This Meyer's parrot is being clicker-trained and asked to walk toward its carer and step up onto a stand. The clicker is sounded as soon as the bird is about to step up.*

trainer clicks as a cue to the bird that a reward is just about to be given if the bird performs the behavior being requested. The clicker is used as a bridge between the verbal command and the reward that will be given on completion of the behavior. Take care with use of a clicker with African and Timneh grays. These birds use their own clicking sound as part of their innate repertoire of calls. When gray parrots click the sound is used as a threat, a warning that the bird may be about to bite if further provoked.

The use of positive reinforcement (rewards) simply provides your bird with the essential motivation to perform the behaviour you are asking for. Once this arrangement is used by

You can get clickers from many good pet stores; some, like this one, even have a variable volume control!

Alert birds will hone in on the reward.

Give the reward without delay.

Give verbal praise at the same time as giving the reward so the bird associates the two things together.

Shaping a behavior

1

2

3

Shaping is a technique whereby you ask your bird to perform increasingly better approximations of a behavior over several stages. Nervous birds will often be very cautious about stepping onto someone's hand and may have had bad experiences associated with contact with human hands in the past. To overcome this you can use this shaping technique. Before starting, you will need to determine two things:
a) What will be your reinforcing reward?
b) What precisely is your target behavior?

Your reward must be something that you know your bird already really likes, perhaps a small food treat. For this example the target behavior is that eventually you would like the bird to step up onto your hand, following your verbal cue for it to do this. At present it may be too nervous to do this, so you might need five or more stages, as described below, when asking your bird to perform this behavior. Perhaps all it will do at present is take food from your hand. This training is usually best done with the bird out on top of its cage, or on a familiar perch, or stand close to the cage. So your initial target behavior can be:

1 *Bird takes two paces toward my right hand (in which I offer a reward) when I say "step up."* During your initial training sessions, all you are asking your bird to do is take at least two steps toward your hand while you offer the reward. When it does this, give the reward and combine this action with verbal praise. When the bird is used to doing this, perhaps after a few sessions on the first day, modify your target behavior a little, to stage two.

2 *Bird takes two paces toward my right hand (in which I offer a reward) while my left hand is in view.* Now you are asking the bird to walk at least two paces toward you while it can see your left hand nearby (this is the hand you will eventually ask it to step onto). Again, when it does walk two paces to you, give the reward promptly and praise the bird. When your bird is comfortable with this stage, go to the next stage.

3 *Bird walks to within 1 inch (2.5 cm) of my left hand while a reward is offered in my right hand.* Place your left hand almost between the bird and your right hand, so the bird has to walk toward it

4

5

to take the reward from your right hand. When your bird walks to within an inch of your left hand, reward and praise it. Next stage...

4 *Bird walks toward you and touches left hand with one or both feet, while reward is offered in right hand.* Reward and praise as above, then it's on to the last stage.

5 *Bird walks onto left hand while reward is offered in right hand.* Reward and praise as above—target behavior achieved.

You can of course vary the number of stages you employ to achieve the final behavior. Very nervous birds will require a much more gradual change, perhaps with seven or eight stages. A more confident bird could be accommodated in three or four stages. The key thing is to work at a pace of careful incremental change that your bird is comfortable with.

Right: *Food rewards work well, but only when the bird is hungry for them. Birds should never be deprived of food generally, but you can certainly restrict some favorite food items on the days you will be training.*

Reading your bird's body language

In addition to using reward-based training as outlined in the applied behavior analysis training methods, you should try to become attuned to your bird's body language, the bird's "moods," and how the bird reacts to things at all times. As mentioned earlier, all parrots have a well-developed "language" that they use for communication. This language can comprise hundreds of different calls, postures and actions that each species will use readily as required. With time, you will get to know how your particular bird shows its likes and dislikes for certain things, and how it shows nervousness or playfulness or interest in

Above: *As well as a range of calls, the "language" of this hyacinth macaw includes many postures and head-bobbing actions.*
Left: *A nervous African gray. Note the feathers held down tightly, the wide staring eyes, and the wings raised in preparation for flight.*

negative behaviors that can be triggered by events that cause the bird to be nervous, fearful or aggressive. Then there are the positive behaviors, which cause the bird to show interest, a liking for something, playfulness or a desire to be sociable.

NERVOUS, ALMOST BY DEFAULT

Most birds show nervousness by backing away from the cause of the problem or leaning away, and the bird will hold its feathers down very tightly. The eyes will be wide and staring, and the bird may prepare to take flight. If the bird is on your hand, you may feel it gripping your finger tightly. When this occurs, you should pause any training session for a few minutes to give the bird time to calm down. Aggression is shown in almost all birds by the bird appearing to make

something. That said, many of the basic behaviors are similar, so it's worth taking a look at them here in general terms.

The behaviors you need to look out for are broadly displayed in two areas. There are

Understanding behavior

itself larger. This is the equivalent of a dog raising the hair along its back. Parrots will do the same, and you will see an aggressive stance when the bird raises the

feathers on its back and neck, though sometimes this pose lasts only for a second or two. The bird will also stare hard at the source of the problem causing this reaction. Birds that are generally bold or confident in their manner show mild aggression quite commonly, and it might sometimes be better interpreted as the bird simply being confident or determined rather than aggressive.

Above: *The raised back feathers show that something has stimulated aggression in this gray.*
Below: *When angry or excited, many parrots will "pin" by contracting their pupils rapidly but briefly.*

Parrots are able to control their iris and you will see them "flash" their eyes. This is also known as "pinning" of the eyes. This signal is complex: it can mean either an aggressive intent or that the bird is positively excited by something. Amazons, macaws and poicephalus parrots, such as Meyer's and Senegals, readily pin their eyes; African grays do it sometimes, but not so commonly. The reason behind the pinning depends on the context and what is happening to the bird at that precise moment, so take care. You can assume that the bird is uninhibited in its behavior. Anything might happen while the bird is pinning its eyes, so it's best to back off for a while and come back a little later, when the bird is more relaxed.

Reading your bird's body language

African and Timneh gray parrots can produce a sharp clicking sound. This is made by snapping the lower bill against the inside of the upper bill, which generates a mechanical "click" each time. This is a clear warning from the bird that it is upset and should not be approached. Another common pose is the fanning of the tail; again macaws, Amazons and some cockatoos do this very readily, and it tells you the bird is simply

Above: *This cockatoo has stretched up to its full height and raised its crest to add emphasis. The bird is very interested in something and likely to be cooperative.*
Left: *Note the flared wings and eye pinning in this excited blue and gold macaw.*

the bird alone for the moment. With cockatoos, any hissing sound should be interpreted as the bird being frightened or aggressive about something, so be aware of the context in which this happens. Is the bird leaning toward something (it likes it, is interested)? Or away from something, and it therefore is nervous of it?

Positive behavior signals to look for in parrots are many and varied. When you have a new bird, after a day or two many of them will begin to recognize you and accept you as a friend. This is shown by a standard greeting posture. Here, the bird raises both wings together over the back as though stretching them. This is the bird's way of saying "Hello" and that it knows who you are.

very excited (negatively or positively so take care). In addition, Amazons and macaws will hold their wings out, exposing the bright red or yellow feathers on the bend of the wing, their "shoulders." Cockatoos will raise their crests at almost any stimulation. It can simply be interpreted as "Hello, here I am," or it can warn you to leave

Understanding behavior

You should respond by saying the bird's name in greeting as well. When birds are in a receptive mood and want to interact, they will often fluff out the feathers on their face, just below the beak, while holding down all other feathers. Also, the eyes may appear sunken in and have a soft look, quite different from the staring, scared expression of a nervous bird (see page 56).

(see page 56).

Left: *Note the partially closed upper eyelid and slightly fluffed facial feathers in this relaxed gray.*

used to human company, like having their heads scratched, and many will ask for this "mutual preening" from their carer. They will request this by lowering the head and fluffing out the facial and head feathers. The eye looks relaxed, even sleepy and sunken while doing this.

Almost all parrots emit a rasping or purring sound by grinding their upper and lower bills together. The birds usually do this when they are relaxed but may not wish to be disturbed. So approach the bird carefully when you hear this. Parrots have a range of "commencement" signals. Commencement signals are given when the bird is preparing to perform some behavior but is still indecisive or lacking in confidence. The bird will look very attentive and may scratch its head or shift its weight from one foot to the other several times. It may turn around on its present perch and prepare (several times) to take flight but not actually move from the perch.

SOFT SOUNDS IN TRUSTING BIRDS

Parrots also use calls that are very soft, indeed almost inaudible unless you are very close to the bird. These are made when the bird is in a good mood. You can help here by also talking quietly in a very soft voice to your bird. All parrots, once tame and

Right: *This gray's head feathers are fluffed up while those lower down remain flattened. The bird is relaxed.*

Training your bird

WHY TRAIN A PARROT?

In order to ensure that a companion parrot gets on well with people, it is vital that the bird's carer and everyone who wants to interact with the bird communicate well with it. This is essential for a

Above: *Parrots watch you, particularly your hands and face, very closely. This gray is being shown some new foods as his carer appears to eat them himself.*

stable relationship to form between the bird and its human family. Therefore, the purpose of training for companion birds is to ensure some basic two-way communication between you and your bird, just as a dog owner needs to have good communication with their animal.

Training parrots does not usually take long. Indeed, with the right methods, most attempts at training will see results within a few days. Also, the age at which training is undertaken does not really matter. Although it is sometimes a little easier to train young birds, parrots of any age can

always be taught new things. Once training is successful, you will be able to ask your bird to do (or not do) several things on request. The bird's compliance is never 100 percent guaranteed, and it would be unrealistic to expect this. However, most parrots will accept requests from their carers most (though not all) of the time. Once a bird has been trained to accept a few requests, it is much easier to live with them out of their cages for most of the time you are together, as they pose fewer problems while out than untrained birds. And birds certainly need to be out of their cages for several hours each day in order not to become frustrated with overuse of the cage. Training also ensures that the bird remains tame and allows you to introduce new things, such as new toys and foods, far more easily. The training is quite easy to achieve with most parrots, but nervous birds will take longer to train. (See pages 62–63 for details on working with nervous birds.)

TAMENESS AND TRAINING

Tameness should not be confused with a bird being trained. A bird that steps onto the hand whenever it wants to is not necessarily trained. Some birds that are indeed tame and confident but untrained can cause problems for their owners due simply to their lack of training.

Most other books that deal with the training of parrots assume that the bird's wings will be clipped, but most owners prefer to avoid wing-clipping their bird. Accordingly, the training described here assumes your bird will be kept without having its wings clipped. Indeed, wing-clipping can cause more problems than it solves, as is discussed on pages 108–111.

Left: *There is no need to wing-clip a bird; instead just teach your parrot certain basic flight requests.*

Above: *Offering a food treat by hand can be the first stage in gaining the trust of a nervous bird.*

Instead of wing-clipping a bird to control it, it just needs to be trained to accept some simple flight commands in addition to being asked to "step up" and "step down" from your hand. The training

methods described below are designed to work by helping you to develop a trusting relationship with your bird by offering rewards for the behaviors you would like to see repeated.

On no account should any parrot ever be punished for any "bad behavior." Once the main principles of behavior are understood, then it can be seen that any punishment will be counterproductive and may well cause more problems than it solves. Even unintentional punishment and admonishment of a bird with verbal reprimands can have adverse effects on parrots and should be avoided. Bold and even aggressive birds are actually far easier to train than nervous ones. Although such birds may bite sometimes, such a problem is not usually difficult to overcome through reward-based training.

Nervous birds

Wild-caught birds used to be imported and sold as pets in the U.K., and some of these wild-caught birds may still be offered for sale. They may be very nervous due to bad experiences with people. Similarly, captive-bred

Above: *Wild sulfur-crested cockatoos. Flight is a bird's innate escape action when startled. Caged birds cannot do this so they often feel trapped and more nervous if something frightens them.*

birds that have had bad experiences with people will be nervous or even afraid, particularly of human hands. Their nervousness may be made worse by their sense of being trapped in a cage. Nervous birds require very careful, sensitive treatment in order to allow them to lose their fear and become tame. Long before any attempt is made to ask a nervous bird to step up onto the hand, you will need to go through a gentle

taming process that may take several weeks. Here, the same principles of rewarding "desired" behaviors are used as in the more formal training sessions, but progress with nervous birds will usually be very slow. Nervous birds should always have a perch in their cage that is higher than your eye level when you are standing next to the cage. This will reduce the bird's fear of people who come close.

To start the taming process you can try the following methods. Sit down below the bird while it is in its cage but not so close that it shows any signs of being afraid of you. It is best to sit side-on to the bird and avoid looking directly at it. Spend a few minutes in this position doing quiet activities, such as reading or eating a snack. Let the bird see you eating your own food: Do not look directly at the bird at first, as this can upset it. Over several sessions, gradually sit closer to the bird, provided your approach does not cause it to be fearful; this may take several days. For parrots, eating is a social activity: when one bird sees another (or a human) eating, it is reassuring. Over time, the bird will get accustomed to these sessions and either eat its own food or show some interest in your food. At this point, offer the bird a favorite tidbit through the bars of the cage.

Later on, as the bird's confidence increases, you can open the cage door and try offering a food treat directly to the bird while it is still in the cage by placing your hand-held tidbit just below its beak, provided it appears likely to accept this. Later still, you can try leaving the cage door open and then offer the bird a treat after it has come out or at least moved toward the open cage door.

1 *This bird has decided to climb down its cage to investigate its carer; its confidence is improving.*

2 *Reward this behavior by immediately offering a food treat to the bird and speak softly to encourage it.*

3 *Later still, the bird now feels confident enough to approach the carer with the cage door opened.*

4 *Again, a well-earned reward is given. This bird is now well on the way to trusting its carer.*

To get it to return, make it obvious that you have put a treat in its food bowl for it when it returns. Encourage it softly as it attempts to do the right thing. Remember, the speed at which you carry out this taming process is determined not by you, but by the bird. How long it takes will depend on how nervous the bird is, as well as on how careful you are in advancing through the taming stages. Once the bird is taking some food treats from your hand, you can start to teach the bird some of the more formal requests as explained further in this section.

Getting started

I n this section, we will be putting into practice the principles of applied behavior analysis discussed earlier, (see pages 48–51). Most birds can be trained in the same room as their cage. However, with a bird that is aggressive when in or near its cage, it may be best to carry out the first sessions of training well away from its cage, perhaps in another room where the bird is much less likely to show aggressive behaviors. Conversely, nervous

Left: *Remove any large mirrors or turn them around so the bird is not confused by reflections.*

hung over them to prevent the bird flying into the glass. There should be no mirrors or ceiling fans in the room. Make sure there are no places where the bird might fly to and land on that are higher than your chest, so remove any pictures or ornaments as necessary before taking the bird to this room. Keep the door closed throughout the training sessions.

Above: *Two chairs placed fairly close together provide all you need as perches for the first training sessions. Make sure they are easy for the bird to grip.*

birds should always be trained near their cage, as this will help them to become more confident in your company. When a training room is used, it is best if it is fairly small—a spare bedroom is usually ideal. It should be carpeted and sparsely furnished with a couple of chairs that you will need to use as perches for the bird. Any large-pane windows should have curtains or net drapes

THE FIRST REQUESTS

All birds should first be asked to accept three requests. These are:

1 "Step up" (means step onto my hand now).
2 "Go down" (means step off my hand now).
3 "Stay" (means do not come on me for now).
Assuming your bird can fly, it should also be taught these requests:
4 "Stay" (do not fly to me for now).
5 "Go" (leave me by flying from me).
6 "Off there" (leave a banned perch by flying off it when asked).
7 "On here" (means fly to me).

TEACHING THE REQUESTS AND USING REWARDS

In order to get the bird to learn easily, it is important to remain calm and confident at all times so that you appear to be someone who never gets flustered, regardless of what happens during training. Your calmness and confidence (even just the outward appearance of it!) will be

Training your bird

sensed by the bird, and this in itself is a great aid when working with any bird. As discussed in the behaviour section, the key to successful training is the use of a reward. Before starting to train your bird, make sure you know what you will be using to reward your bird's good behavior. The reward must be something that your particular bird already really likes. If you are using a food reward, you may need to experiment with various items to determine what your bird's favored treat really is. While some birds work very well for a favorite food treat, others may prefer to have their head gently scratched or to be given a favorite small toy. On training days it is sensible to prevent the bird having free access to whatever rewards you will be using. This will

increase the bird's motivation for these rewards. During training sessions make sure the bird only gets these rewards after having actually earned them: don't give free rewards or the bird will have no incentive to cooperate.

Above: *Some parrots are easily motivated by a favorite toy. This Meyer's finds a small ball irresistible.*

Above: *Your hand should be your bird's perch when it is with you. Keep your fingers in line and your thumb out of the way with the bird facing you.*

Above: *This is not the way to hold a bird! Here, the thumb is sticking up and is provocative; this hand posture should be avoided.*

The first requests

The bird should be in a calm receptive mood before any training. With the bird in position, perhaps on the back of a chair, and the door to the room closed, you will be ready to make a start. Approach the bird and try to make eye contact, perhaps by saying its name. Make sure it is attentive before you interact with it. Show the bird the reward you are going to give it and put this up to your own mouth a few times to attract the bird's attention. With your reward held in one hand, offer your other hand as a perch for the bird to step up onto. Next, raise your step-up hand a bit higher than the bird's feet and approach it calmly. Try to maintain eye contact to keep its attention. The step-up hand should be held with the thumb down and your four fingers in line. Place your hand so it is almost touching the bird's feet near its belly and say "Step up." You can also gently touch the bird's belly with the edge of your forefinger. Most birds will step onto your finger after a few attempts. When it does so, praise it verbally and, after only a few seconds, ask it to "Go down" and set it back down onto the same place from where it stepped up and give your reward at once. When setting the bird back down, take it close to the perch so it is facing it and say "Go down," perhaps allowing the bird's chest just to touch the chair back. Birds tend to step up onto a perch that is just above the level of their feet more easily than they step down onto a lower perch.

ALWAYS REMAIN CALM

If a bird bites when you are training it, try not to show any reaction; in particular do not say anything. Try to remain calm and simply repeat

1 *Show your bird the reward it can earn and be sure that this is something your bird already really likes.*

4 *Asking the bird to "Go down." It helps to point at or even touch the requested perch with your other hand.*

your request in a calm voice. If the bird flies down to the floor, do not chase around after it. Allow it a few moments to calm down, then kneel down beside it and place your hand just above its feet and repeat the request to "step up" while you show the reward in your other hand. Many birds will actually step up very easily from the floor. When it does step up, praise it, then set it back

2 *Parrots watch your hands and face carefully. Put the reward up to your own mouth to encourage interest.*

3 *When asking for a "Step up" your hand should be close to the bird with the thumb down, out of the way.*

5 *The bird is just leaving the hand here and will turn around to face you when securely on the perch.*

6 *Give your rewards for both commands promptly and make sure the bird has plenty of time to enjoy them.*

down on the perch you started from and give it its reward.

Allow the bird plenty of time to eat the food reward and use encouraging words as it does so. It often helps if you eat something yourself—when the bird sees you eating, it helps stimulate it to eat as well. If this is all you achieve during the first lesson, you will have made a good start. It is best

to finish each session on a good note. Training sessions should be quite short; three to five minutes is long enough. On the first day you might only have one session, but on succeeding days you can build up to two or three sessions. If, during any training sessions, the bird appears upset, end the session immediately and allow the bird time to calm down.

A few hints on "step up" requests

1 *This gray is being asked to step up onto a stick in much the same way it is asked to step onto your hand.*

2 *Here the trainer touches the "go down" perch with his other hand as a cue to the bird to leave him.*

3 *When bringing a bird to a "step off" perch, hold the stick just below the level of the perch.*

If you have high ceilings or places where your bird can get out of reach, it is also a good idea to train it to step on and off a stick held in your hand. Stick training is also useful for birds that are either afraid of hands or inclined to bite hands severely. The stick-perch should be similar to a perch in the bird's cage, but make sure it is thin enough so that the bird can grip it easily by wrapping its toes right around it. It should be presented to the bird as a perch, just above the level of its feet, never pointed at the bird. Just give the "step up" request as you present the stick, then set the bird back down again and reward it immediately as before.

Most birds soon learn to step up and step down from the hand or a stick, though some may be slow or reluctant to learn at first. But as soon as the bird knows

Right: *Always give your reward without any delay, otherwise the bird may not make the connection between the action you are teaching it and the reward itself.*

Training your bird

Far left and left: *This Amazon, who is already good at stepping up and down to the hand, is being taught to step from one hand to the other. Note that the receiving hand is always held slightly higher than the leaving hand, as birds find it easier to step up to a perch than to step down to one.*

that it will receive a desirable reward for complying with your requests, it is likely to cooperate quickly. By having a few regular sessions you should find you make considerable progress quite soon. Be sure to praise all good behavior in an enthusiastic tone of voice at the same time as you offer any other reward you intend to use. Soon, both you and the bird should be working together more easily and doing these things automatically, but do not rush things; go at a pace that you know is comfortable for your bird.

When the bird is proficient at these first requests, you should then use these verbal cues for it to step up and step down every time you wish the bird to step on or off your hand, and not just during training sessions. Anyone else who works with the bird should also use exactly the same words and hand gestures for the same requests, otherwise the bird may become confused. If you have been using a training room, once the bird learns the requests there (at least the "step up" and "go down" requests) you

can then repeat this process with the bird in the same room as its cage.

BEGINNING TO BOND WITH THE TRAINER

It is useful to be able to get a bird used to being transferred from one hand to the other, again using the "step up" phrase as you ask for this. It is best to prevent a bird from developing the habit of walking up your arm onto your shoulder. Shoulder birds may object to being trained, so when the bird is with you, make a point of carrying it around perched on your hand as taught in the training sessions. During the training process, most birds begin to bond with the trainer as they agree to accept the requests and get rewards for their cooperation. When this happens you will have made great progress and begun to acquire that effective communication that is so vital for you and your bird to have with each other. When the bird has learned to accept stepping up and down from your hand, you'll be ready to teach it the other requests that follow.

The "stay" requests

When your bird is good at stepping on and off your hand, you should no longer need to use a training room for the next requests. You should be able to teach these in the same room as the bird's cage. Indeed, you can teach "stay" in a fairly informal atmosphere, while the bird is with you but out of its cage. As when teaching the earlier requests, it is vital that you reward the bird whenever it tries to do the right thing in

place for long periods, since this can result in serious behavioral problems as seen with some stand-trained birds. In order to ask a bird to refrain from approaching you for the moment, perhaps as it is walking toward you, try to make eye contact and raise one hand with your palm facing the bird and say "Stay." This gesture will cause most birds to pause in their movements. Praise and reward the bird when it stops.

Above: *This gesture asks the bird not to approach the trainer. Note the reward to be given if the bird stays.*

Above: *Again, give your reward for correct behavior promptly and move back as the bird enjoys it.*

order to give it the incentive to agree with your requests. Teaching "stay" is just a way of letting your bird know that sometimes there are occasions when it cannot approach you, perhaps when you are leaving the room but cannot take the bird with you.

The "stay" request does not mean the bird should simply "stay where it is," but only that it should not come to you for the moment. Indeed, parrots should be encouraged to be active birds and certainly should not be forced to stay in one

DO NOT FLY TO ME

Once trained, birds will often want to fly to you and land on you. This, of course, is fine on most occasions, but there will be times when you may not want the bird to come to you, perhaps when you have to leave the room without having the bird with you. Here, you can use the "stay" request and hand gesture so that you can ask the bird to refrain from flying to you. If the bird disobeys and flies toward you, keep your hand held up and say "Stay" again while you prevent it from landing on you, using your raised hand as a barrier between you and the bird. You can also raise your other hand as well in the same gesture. The bird will soon learn to turn around and land elsewhere. When it does, praise and reward it promptly and then leave the room, closing the door behind you as you check that the bird is not trying to follow you.

"Stay" is a very important request and helps the bird to understand when it can and cannot come to you. Whenever you leave a room while your bird is out of the cage, always check to see what it is doing, particularly as you go through the doorway. Trained flying birds will often want to follow you, but take care to use the "stay" request to prevent the bird colliding with the door as it closes behind you. "Stay" can also be useful to stop a bird flying to a place that might be unsuitable or dangerous for it to land on.

Top right: *Use the same gesture if a bird flies toward you and you wish to prevent it from landing on you.*
Opposite right: *You may need to use both hands to make sure that you prevent the bird from landing on you.*

This Timneh gray loves a head-scratch as a reward during training sessions.

First flight requests

You won't find information about these requests in any other pet parrot book, but since birds fly (and should be encouraged to do so) it is important to teach companion parrots these requests. Before teaching flight requests, the bird should have at least reasonable flying skills and be able to land with some control. If your bird is not very good at flying, perhaps while it is still waiting to regrow its main flight feathers if it was previously wing-clipped, you should wait until it is better at flying before teaching these requests.

"GO" (FLY OFF ME)

This request is used to ask the bird to fly off you and land on another familiar place. Initially, teach this request by standing with the bird perched on your hand 3 or 4 feet (about 1 m) from its cage or any other place that the bird is already used to perching on. Have a reward conspicuously in view at the place you will be asking the bird to fly to.

Normally when the bird is on your hand it should be facing you so that you can maintain eye contact and read its body language. But for this "go" request, you should turn your hand at the wrist so the bird is facing away from you and toward the familiar perch. At the same time, use your other hand, held lower down, to point to the place you want the bird to fly to. Then say "Go, go" and swing the hand with the bird on gently but decisively in the direction of the perch or cage on which your bird's reward is situated. The bird should leave you and land on the perch/cage top. As soon as it does, praise it as it takes its reward. When he is happy to fly from this short distance, gradually increase the distance to the perch.

Later, practice this request in other locations until you can ask the bird to leave you wherever you happen to be. If the bird flies off you having been asked to "go" and tries to return by landing on you, you can use the "stay" request to prevent this. The aim of the "go" request is to ask the bird

1   2   3   4

1. Normally, a bird should be perched on your hand facing you. 2. But when asking a bird to "go" turn your hand, so the bird faces away from you. 3. Then, use *your other hand to point in the direction you'd like the bird to fly to as you say, "Go go." 4. The bird should fly to the intended perch, and promptly get his reward.*

Training your bird

Below: *It is not recommended that a parrot be allowed to stay on your shoulder if it lands there, as you cannot read the bird's body language or predict its behaviors without making eye contact with it. This bird will be asked to leave by flying off.*

The bird should leave by flying to another suitable perch and not return to the trainer once asked to leave.

Birds on a shoulder can inflict serious bites to the face merely in a moment of over-excitement.

Above right: *The trainer says "Go, go"and then jerks his shoulder in the direction in which he would like the bird to fly. If, after leaving the shoulder, the parrot tries to return to you, use the "stay" command to prevent it from landing on you.*

to fly off you and perch on another place and not come back to you. Once you have trained the bird to fly off your hand on command, you can use the same phrase to ask it to leave your shoulder by flying off. To do this, just say "Go, go" and then jerk your shoulder sharply upward while aiming the bird in the direction of a familiar perch. Again, if it tries to return to you just after you give the "go" request, use the "stay" command to prevent it from landing on you.

Once the bird is accustomed to you using these commands initially in familiar places, you should then be able to ask your bird to leave you wherever you happen to be with it. However, it is important to start teaching this request in places that are already familiar to the bird. These sessions should be very brief; initially, just make one or two attempts at teaching this until the bird is used to accepting this request. Then try using "go" at other locations.

Further flight commands

"Off there!"

THE "OFF THERE" REQUEST

This request is mainly used as a safety request to ask a bird to leave any place where it might be dangerous for it to remain, such as the TV, a light fixture or a high perch, such as the top of a door, a curtain rod or anyone's head. This is not the easiest request to teach some birds, but it is very useful to teach your bird the difference between acceptable places for it to land on and banned places it should never use. It also helps to ensure that your bird can fly safely in the home. When the bird does land on an unsuitable place, approach it and make eye contact by saying the bird's name. Then wave one or both hands at the bird in a gesture that is unfamiliar to it as you say "off there." You can also try waving an unfamiliar but harmless object near the bird, such as a handkerchief. The bird should leave this place and then fly to any other familiar place, such as a chair, cage or stand. The bird should not be allowed to fly and land on you as it leaves a banned perch, but instead somewhere else that is safe. When it does land on a familiar perch, praise and reward it as usual, but do not offer too strong a reward. If you do, you may end up actually encouraging the bird to go to a banned perch so as to get a reward after you tell it to leave! The teaching of this "off there" request cannot be preplanned; you will just need to start to teach it if and when your bird lands on unsafe or unacceptable places. Make sure you and

Below left: *Parrots sometimes land on unsuitable or unsafe places. This gray has landed on a houseplant.*
Below center: *It is asked to leave by flying off and going to a suitable perch instead. When* giving the request, do so quite calmly, as you should not get the bird too excited.
Right: *A waved handkerchief helps reinforce the command. Praise the bird when it lands on a suitable perch.*

Training your bird

immediately each time that it already flies to you. Working with the bird when it is about to come to you anyway is a good way to get it used to associating your verbal request "on here" with it coming to you by flight. It is best to start by only asking the bird to fly a short distance to you, so have it 3 or 4 feet (about 1 m) away at first. Each time you see the bird about to fly to you, hold your arm out, and say "On here" and offer a reward that it can see you holding in your hand (again this might be a favorite food treat or favored toy). Give it the reward as soon as it lands and

Above, right and below:
This Timneh gray is asked to fly to the trainer, and the bird's motivation is increased by offering a very tempting reward that is held in the trainer's other hand. The bird is given the reward immediately on landing on the proffered hand.

others in your family are consistent about the places your bird can and cannot use as perches, otherwise the bird may be confused about where it can and cannot fly to.

"ON HERE" (FLY TO ME)

This is a recall request, asking your bird to fly to you on command. By the time you have taught the requests previously described, your bird will probably have bonded quite well to you. Indeed, most trained birds want to be with their trainers and on their hand most of the time. However, you can reinforce the bird's desire to come to you on a verbal command by rewarding it

combine this with enthusiastic verbal praise, perhaps scratching its head as well if it likes this already. Allow the bird plenty of time to enjoy any food reward.

Some informal requests

Whenever you want to give your bird a familiar object or treat to take in its beak, avoid holding the object above your bird's head. Parrots are very wary of hands that are held above them and this may startle them. Instead, make a point of offering the object at beak level or just under the beak. If you name the object at the same time, many birds will learn to associate the name with the object correctly. Each time you offer your bird an object, you can say "Take this" or "Take toy" or "Take nut" as appropriate. Take care when offering a bird any new unfamiliar object. In this case, always make sure

is more likely to take it from you. The use of a spoken phrase while offering an object also tells the bird clearly that you would like it to take it from you. You should be quite relaxed about this request; it does not matter if the bird refuses an object from you since that is its choice.

AVOID CONFRONTATION

If the bird ever picks up an object that might be unsuitable or dangerous and you try to remove it forcibly, the bird's natural reaction will be to hold on to it even more tightly, bite down on it or fly off with it. In this emergency situation you can

Above left and right: *This Meyer's parrot is being asked to take a new toy, but the trainer handles the toy first and puts it up to his own mouth before offering it to the bird.*

to let the bird see you handling the new item first and, especially important, putting it up to your mouth a few times before asking the bird to take it. When a parrot sees you putting an object up to your mouth this tends to reassure it; it tells it that the object is something safe to touch, so it

either offer the bird something else quickly, saying "Take this" (as explained at right), or ask the bird to release its grip on the object by saying "Drop it" as you stand nearby. In the latter case, make sure to keep your hands out of the way until the object has been dropped. Then reward and praise the bird for its compliance. Teaching these requests and using them as needed is far better than actually trying to remove an object from the bird's beak since it is much less confrontational.

Training your bird

It is of course best to avoid confrontation at all times when working with parrots. Any forceful use of speech or excited gesticulations are only likely to result in the bird getting even more excited, and invariably this will make matters worse. It is also better to avoid the use of the word "no." Many people use this word too frequently and too aggressively, and its effect is soon lost on the bird. When your bird is out of the cage, you need to be attentive to it at all times. When some mischievous behavior is about to happen you can often check this by simply saying the bird's name in a calm tone of voice, perhaps followed by saying "Be careful" while maintaining eye contact with the bird. This just lets the bird know you are aware of what it might be about to do and that you wish it to refrain from doing so. Your calm tone of voice and maintenance of eye contact will often forestall the unwanted act without the bird getting overexcited.

Below: *This Meyer's parrot has picked up a china cup. It is better to be vigilant and avoid situations like this in the first place.*

There's many a slip 'twixt cup and beak!

Above: *This bird has taken hold of a pen. It could get into an awful mess with ink all over itself if left unattended, and the pen may also be ruined.*

Left: *When your bird has taken something it should not have, calmly ask it to "Drop it" and praise it when it does so. Don't try to take the object away by hand—the bird is liable to hang on more tightly.*

Other training hints

Sometimes parrots may be forcibly held by a trainer who keeps the bird on the hand by covering the bird's toes with the thumb. Parrots should not be forced to stay on you by this method. If a parrot attempts to fly while being held by its feet, it can result in painful dislocation of the bird's toes or other joints. Occasionally, even when trained, your bird may leave you without being told to go; it is best to be fairly relaxed about this and just ask the bird to "step up" again a few minutes later if you need to.

There are two ways in which a bird can be restrained safely, perhaps when you need to check the bird's condition. The first involves asking the bird to "go down" on your chest. Have the bird perched on your hand as usual, facing you, but place your other hand over the bird's back as you say "Go down" and draw the bird to your chest while you withdraw the hand it was perching on. The bird will grip your clothing as it releases its grip on your hand. Then reward

the bird with a gentle head scratch using your free hand. You can then approach a familiar perch (or the cage) and set the bird down saying "Go down" as you release and reward it. Often it is best to practice this request and set the bird down on various familiar places before using this method to return a bird to its cage. In this way the bird will not associate it with having to go back to the cage, and this will make the request easier to use when you need to put the bird in the cage without delay.

The second method involves the use of a towel. Here, "toweling" a bird should not be confused with the practice of forcibly wrapping a bird up in a towel to "train" or tame it. Such enforced toweling is not appropriate at all. However, it is useful to get your bird used to being held gently in a towel, and it makes it easier for birds to be checked by a vet. Once the bird is trained in the requests as explained earlier, you can practice having it held in a

Below: *The "go down" onto chest restraint. **1.** Hold the bird on your hand as usual, facing you. **2.** Then bring the bird to your chest. **3.** Cover its back with your* other hand. ***4.*** *Reward the bird, perhaps with a gentle head-scratch. **5.** Then release it onto a suitable perch.*

1

2

3

Training your bird

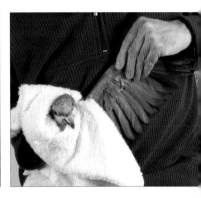

towel. Use a towel of a bland or neutral color, such as white or cream. Dark- or bold-colored towels may frighten your bird. To introduce the bird to the towel gradually, start by having the bird on your lap and offer it the corner of the towel to play with or to chew on. After a few such sessions, let more of the towel come into contact with the bird's body. Eventually you should be able to accustom the bird to being held gently in the towel so you can restrain it for a few brief minutes. Reward the bird and encourage it at all times by giving praise or head scratches.

Above left to right: *This Amazon is being gently restrained in a towel; the process should be taught gradually until the bird is familiar with being toweled.*

HARNESSES

No type of leg restraint should be used on a parrot, as any pulling can result in the leg being dislocated. Although most parrots dislike anything touching their feathers, some will accept a harness that can be used, with

care, to take your bird outdoors. This is fitted around the body with a strap held below to hold onto. Birds will need to be properly trained, with care, if they are to accept a harness. Introduce the harness very gradually. On the first few occasions make sure the bird only wears the harness for a few seconds and do this in a familiar place indoors. If the bird seems comfortable with this, gradually increase the time that the bird wears the harness at each session. If at any stage the bird does not seem comfortable after a few trials, do not persist with forcing it on a bird. Instead, consider building a day-flight cage or aviary.

4   5

Teaching a bird to talk—mimicry

Part of the popularity of parrots is due to their abilities to imitate human speech. Many parrots are often referred to as "good talkers." African and Timneh gray parrots are particularly well known for the accuracy of their speech reproduction. They can pick up the accent and inflections of the individual they are copying, though gray parrots are often reluctant to talk in the company of strangers. Amazon parrots often talk very well, and they are more inclined than gray parrots to talk in the company of strangers, but the quality of their voice is not as good as the grays. Smaller birds, such as budgies and cockatiels, can also imitate speech, but these birds have a smaller, rather squeaky tone to their voices.

This type of "speech" is, of course, generally merely mimicry. It is only mimicry because the bird has not been taught to use the words in their proper context. Unlike any other companion animal, parrots are quite capable of using human speech in its proper context, but this requires the teacher to teach the bird to use words in the correct context in the first place. In using mere mimicry parrots will often copy sounds that are associated with dramatic actions. So they are very likely to copy swearing when this is associated with extravagant gestures and a raised voice. They are also likely to copy familiar, regular sounds when an action follows. These can include the sound of the door bell, smoke alarm, microwave and phone. In all these cases, the bird will see someone reacting to the sound, and so it will be inclined to make the sound, itself, simply to get a reaction. Parrots are often very good at calling the dog and telling people off in a firm voice.

Parrots will commonly mimic the sound of a phone ringing.

UNWANTED MIMICRY

Although we might naturally find these things amusing to start with, the repetitive, unwanted copying of some sounds can cause real problems to some parrot owners. Where the noise is at a high volume then there is the risk that your neighbors might complain as well.

Left: *When any sound occurs in combination with a specific action, the bird is more likely to mimic the sound and may do so repeatedly to provoke a reaction.*

Training your bird

Right: *When parrots imitate humans, unwanted actions may occur, such as when a parrot calls the pet dog by its name. Take great care here; this may seem amusing, but parrots and dogs should never be left unsupervised, even if they are allowed to be together.*

will often result in the bird copying you through its inclination to mimic sounds generally. It can be useful to get a bird to say its own name, and some owners teach birds to say their own addresses as well. This can help to recover a lost or even stolen bird. There have been court cases concerning stolen parrots in which the vocal repertoire of the bird has been used as evidence of its true ownership, and the bird returned to its rightful home.

Below: *Repeating a word or phrase will often get your bird to mimic it in mere "parrot" fashion, without associating the words with any meaning. But take care what you say in front of a parrot; your words may come back to haunt you sooner than you think!*

Mimicry in parrots is most common in those birds that are kept as pets, particularly birds that are kept on their own without the company of other parrots. When parrots do enjoy the company of other parrotlike birds, they tend to keep to parrot sounds rather than human speech. Where solitary birds are copying sounds, including speech, this may be simply a means for the bird to enrich its own life by entertaining itself. So, if you wish to encourage your bird to speak, simply repeating a common short phrase

Speaking in context

Instead of asking a bird merely to mimic human speech, it is not difficult to train it to use speech in its proper context. This certainly takes the notion of the much-needed two-way communication between you and your bird to a higher level. To teach meaningful speech to a bird you simply use an approach similar to the one you would with a very young child. Each time you give your bird an object that you know it is interested in, such as a toy or food treat, repeat the name of the object in a clear voice, saying "Peanut" or "Grape" or "Toy" as appropriate. After a while, many birds will realize that the name refers to the object, and your bird may then use the correct name for the object when it wishes to have it.

Left: Naming an object as you give it to your bird increases its chances of using speech in context.

Above: *Cockatoos can reproduce many new sounds, but they often do so at such a volume that it causes real problems for both owners and their neighbors.*

The bird may also use the right word for objects that are not in view at the time. Here, you should assume the bird wants the named object and offer it if you can. Parrots may also use speech to make requests and may even use the verbal requests you have been asking your bird to accept. It is not uncommon for parrots to say "Step up" when they are in their cage and wish to come out. You should respond appropriately, either saying "Yes, step up" as you get the bird out, or telling the bird that it cannot come out for now.

MODEL/RIVAL TEACHING METHOD

Professor Irene Pepperberg has been working with gray parrots in the U.S. for many years. Her birds use hundreds of words and phrases to request items and answer questions. The birds

Training your bird

can respond correctly to questions about an object's size, shape, color, the type of material it is made from and the number of objects on display. These parrots show abilities similar to a human toddler learning to use speech. Professor Pepperberg

Left: *Professor Irene Pepperberg's work with gray parrots has made a huge contribution to our understanding of the intelligence of these birds.*

uses a method known as the model/rival technique. In the situation described below, two trainers sit next to the bird and exchange objects between themselves, naming or describing the objects each time. After three or four sessions each day over several weeks, the birds can learn to label and describe objects. This technique makes use of the bird's natural inclination to want to join in the activity, as the bird is encouraged to use speech. Below is a typical sample of dialogue between Alex, an African gray, and his two trainers, Irene and Bruce. In this session, Alex is already familiar with the objects but his pronunciation of the word "five" is poor, so the trainers are trying to improve the bird's pronunciation so he can clearly label a bundle of five pieces of small wooden craft sticks.

Irene (holding the five sticks): Bruce, what's this?
Bruce: Five wood.
Irene: That's right, five wood. Here you are…
(Hands the five wooden sticks to Bruce. Bruce begins to break one apart, much as Alex would.)
Alex: ii wood. ⸳
Bruce (to Alex): Better. (Meaning say the word "five" with better pronunciation as Bruce shows

him the five sticks again.)
How many?
Alex: No! (Alex refuses to cooperate.)
Bruce (turns from Alex to establish contact with Irene): Irene, what's this? (Presents sticks.)
Irene (imitating Alex's poor pronunciation):
ii wood.
Bruce (to Irene): Better…how many?
Irene: Five wood (takes sticks), five wood (faces Alex). How many wood?
Alex: Fife wood.
Irene: OK, close enough, five wood… Here's five wood. (Gives sticks to Alex.)

Above: *Alex, one of Irene Pepperberg's grays, at work on a lesson on the labeling of colors. This bird has a vocabulary of hundreds of words.*

Your parrot's home

CAGES

It is often said that a parrot's cage is its home but, unless you live entirely in a one-room apartment, this is a poor comparison. The bird's home should comprise much more than its cage. Many behavioral problems are caused simply by the fact that a bird as intelligent as a parrot is often expected to stay in its cage for most of the daytime, perhaps being let out for a few hours only each day. If dogs and cats were housed in this way, we would expect to see behavioral problems, and the same can easily occur with any parrot.

In general, the smaller the cage the less time a bird should spend in it. Cages for medium to larger parrots are often so small that they

Left: *This cage is not quite big enough for the cockatoos inside. It would be just big enough for an African gray.*

actually prevent the birds within from being able to fly. Where such a small cage is used, the bird will need to be out of it most of the day if behavioral problems are to be prevented. It is better if you can offer your bird accommodation that is large enough for it to fly in and use a big flight cage or an indoor aviary. The main aspect to bear in mind regarding the size of your bird's cage is the bird's wingspan. This can be surprisingly large, usually more than twice the length of the bird's body. To measure your own bird's wingspan, just have someone hold it gently, perhaps in a towel, with one wing outstretched and measure from the center of the bird's back to the tip of the fully opened wing, then double that measurement; that is the wingspan. An Amazon or African gray has a wingspan of around 28 inches (70 cm) and even a little Meyer's parrot and cockatiels have a wingspan of about 16 inches (40 cm).

THE BIGGER THE BETTER

For the smaller birds it is possible to find cages that are big enough to induce flight. Here, a cage that is over 3 feet (1 m) wide and 2 feet (60 cm) deep is suitable. The height of the cage is of little importance to the bird, since it will spend very little time in the lower half. However,

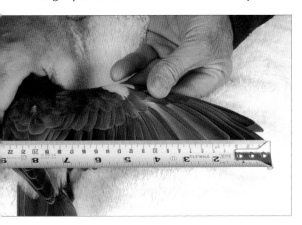

Above: *Determining a bird's wingspan. The distance from this Meyer's parrot's wing tip to the center of its back is 8 in. (20 cm), so the wingspan is 16 in. (40 cm).*

the height should always be such that it allows the bird to fully extend and flap its wings. As a guide, cage height for these smaller birds should be at least 2 feet (60 cm).

For the larger species, such as grays, Amazon parrots and cockatoos, providing a flight cage may require you to convert part of a room into an aviary. For these birds the aviary or flight cage would need to be at least 6 feet (2 m) long to induce flight, and a width of 3 feet (1 m) would allow room for the bird's full wingspan. If you do use a normal, smaller cage, which is not roomy enough to allow flight, you will need to ensure that the bird spends most of the day out of its cage. The large macaws, such as the scarlet, blue and gold, and green-winged, need much more space and should have their own room measuring at least 10 square feet (3 m²) to allow

Above: *Spherical cages are confusing for birds. Both the bar spacing and size of this cage mean it is not suitable for any bird.*
Left: *These cages are of sound construction with both vertical and horizontal bars. The smaller one would suit a small conure, the larger one an Amazon.*

them to exercise properly. Whatever type of cage or aviary you provide, the bird will need to come out and spend several hours each day with you for company and be encouraged to fly during this time as well.

Cage furnishings

Parrots like to climb, so it is best to have a cage that has plenty of horizontal bars rather than just vertical bars, as this makes climbing easier. The cage should be of a strong construction so that the bars cannot be bent or damaged by the bird. Flimsy bars can be bent or damaged and the bird may ingest the coatings. Cages with plastic-coated bars are not suitable for parrots. The highest quality cages are made from stainless steel, but most are made from mild steel with a finish of colored stove-enameled paint. For the safety of the bird it is vital that the spacing between the bars should always be small enough to prevent the bird from poking its head out of

Above: *A triple swing feeder with strong stainless steel bowls, each about 5 in. (13 cm) in diameter.*

Above: *Cockatoo in dangerous housing. This bird could seriously injure itself due to the wide mesh spacing.*

the cage. For small species a bar spacing of ½ inch (1.3 cm) will be needed. Medium-sized birds, such as grays and Amazons, will need a bar spacing of 1 inch (2.5 cm) and for large macaws the spacing can be up to 1 ½ inches (3.8 cm). Some cages are made from clear plastic with no bars at all. However, such construction prevents

the birds from climbing and is not recommended. It is best if the cage is fitted with several swing feeders, which allows you to change the food pots from outside the cage.

Usually, the top perch in the cage should not be higher than your eye level when you are standing next to it, but nervous birds should always have a top perch that is above your eye level. You can always reduce the height of an excessively tall cage by sawing a few inches off the legs (and replacing the castors if these have been fitted). Some cages are fitted with a grill on the floor just above the base tray. The grill prevents the bird from retrieving dropped items and may cause injuries if the bird panics in the night and crash-lands with its legs through the bars. It should be removed and the floor covered with newspaper, which must be changed daily. To help the bird feel more secure, cages should have a solid back instead of bars on all sides. Since it is hard to find parrot cages with a solid back, the cage should simply be placed with its back against a solid wall.

THE CORRECT SIZE OF PERCH
Bird's feet have a locking mechanism that allows them to grip a perch with minimal use of their

Your parrot's home

feet muscles. However, this only works if the perches are thin enough so the bird can wrap its toes almost right around the perch. Often the perches supplied with a cage are too thick for the bird's feet, so these should be replaced with thinner perches made from natural, untreated hardwood branches with the bark left on. Avoid plastic perches and softwood (pine, spruce), as

these have a gluelike resin that may stick to the

Left: The variable width and narrow diameter of rough, natural perches ensures a good grip.

bird's feathers. A stout rope perch made of natural fibers, such as cotton or hemp, is a good investment. Perches get dirty very quickly, so they should be washed frequently and renewed regularly. It's worth having two sets of perches for each cage so you always have some clean ones whenever you need them.

Your bird's food pots should be big enough to allow the bird to pick out its favorite food items without spilling

Right: *This perch is too thick. The rosella cannot grip this perch properly with its feet, only stand on it.*

Above: *The flexibility of rope perches, and the fact that they can swing about, helps to allow some exercise and can stimulate the bird to play as well.*

other food. It is best to give a bird either one very large food pot or two smaller food pots. A large pot for an African gray or Amazon parrot should be about 5 inches (13 cm) wide. Where two smaller pots are used, these should be about 4 inches (10 cm) wide. Water pots can be smaller.

Furnishing the cage

Most parrots will greatly appreciate having access to a roosting box in their cage. The box should be similar to an ordinary nesting box but with a large entrance hole. It should be slightly larger than the bird in question, big enough to allow the bird to turn around easily

Above: *Many parrots, especially those without the company of any other birds, greatly benefit from having a roosting box like this in their cage.*

inside. For an African gray or Amazon, the internal dimensions of the box should be about 12 square inches x 6 inches high (30 cm² x 15 cm). For a smaller bird, such as a Meyer's parrot, the box should be about 7 square inches x 4 inches high (17.5 cm² x 10 cm). The box should be made from good quality ¾-inch (20 mm) plywood and secured firmly near the top of the cage. If you have a small cage, to save space you can hang the box on the outside, but cut off some of the cage bars so the bird can gain entry from within the cage. Put wood

shavings and some small destructible toys inside for the bird to chew. Access to a box like this gives birds a sense of security and helps them become more confident. Also, parrots will not make any loud calls or scream when inside their box, so it helps in reducing noise problems.

PROVIDE A VARIETY OF TOYS

Toys are an essential aspect of environmental enrichment for your bird. Some toys should be small disposable foot toys that the bird can hold in its foot while it plays with them or tears them apart. Most of them can be acquired at no cost at all. Corks, pine cones, untreated wood, cardboard strips, untreated leather strips and wooden clothes pegs all make good chewable toys for birds. You can also use short lengths of untreated cord made from cotton or hemp, and some birds enjoy playing with bunches of keys. Where toys are hung up, these should always be secured on a very short length of chain or natural fiber cord to avoid the risk of the bird becoming entangled in them. Other toys can be larger and more

Left and above: *These small "foot toys" are often a favorite with parrots. You can devise your own from items around the home or buy them ready-made.*

Your parrot's home

Natural materials include raffia and palm leaves.

Make sure the chain has welded links.

permanent and hung up in the cage. It pays to have a collection of these and change them one at a time every few days to maintain the bird's interest. If you have any ring-shaped toys, take care with the size of the rings. For the safety of the bird, the rings should either be so small that the bird cannot get its head through them, or so large that it can easily pass its whole body through them.

The cage should not be too cluttered up with large toys; three or four of these should suffice. Mirrors are best avoided as they can induce behavioral problems in some birds, though nervous birds may appreciate a mirror until they

Above: *These are ideal hanging toys, made largely out of relatively soft, chewable, natural materials such as cotton, hardwood and raffia. Have several of these types of toy, and change those in the cage occasionally to keep your bird interested in them.*

become tame. Your bird should also have at least one stand on which it can spend some time while out of the cage. The free-standing types (which may have castors attached) should be as large and interesting a stand as you can afford and have several perches, toys and a large food bowl. Small, portable tabletop stands are also invaluable and allow you to have the bird with you in a variety of other places.

An outdoor aviary

Companion birds will benefit greatly from having access to a day-flight—an aviary in the garden that they can use during the daytime in good weather. To encourage the bird to exercise by flying, the aviary needs to be big enough to induce flight. For birds such as Senegals or cockatiels an aviary 8 feet long x 5 feet deep x 6½ feet high (2.5 m x 1.5 m x 2 m) would suffice. For birds the size of an African gray or Amazon parrot the day-flight should be nearly twice this size. The frame can be made of wood and the wire should be strong enough for

Above: *Most cockatoos (and macaws) need a metal-framed aviary, as they can chew through most timber.*

the intended birds. The gauge of the wire relates to its thickness. The lower the gauge number the thicker and stronger the wire. For most medium-sized parrots the wire gauge should be 14 or 12, and the mesh should be 1 square inch (2.5 cm²). For smaller birds, you can use 16 gauge with 1 x ½ inch (2.5 x 1.25 cm) mesh.

Use best quality galvanized mesh, not cheaper hot-dipped mesh; its rough zinc coating can be picked off and eaten by the birds and is poisonous. To deter rats the wire should be buried 12 inches (30 cm) deep in the soil, or the structure can be mounted on a concrete base.

PROVIDE PLENTY OF PLANTS

A sloping roof allows rainwater to drain off easily. Use polycarbonate sheeting for the solid roof sections. This is often used on conservatory roofs and is much stronger than corrugated plastic sheeting. The back can be 7–8 feet (2.1–2.5 m) high with the front about 6½ feet (2 m) high. The back should be made from some solid, opaque material so the bird cannot see through it. Alternatively, build the aviary against a wall. If you use wood, you'll need to cover it with wire mesh to prevent the bird from chewing through it. The design and positioning of the aviary should allow some sun and rain to fall on it, but part of it should be sheltered from this, so your bird can move around to wherever it feels comfortable. Despite coming from tropical countries, parrots dislike spending long periods in direct sunlight, as this causes them to overheat, so ensure the bird always has access to plenty of shade.

Climbing plants, such as clematis, honeysuckle or passion flower, can be grown outside the aviary and encouraged to spread onto the roof. This gives a dappled shade effect and allows the birds to feel more secure since they can hide from hawks or other large birds that they may see flying above them. The aviary should be fitted with natural branches for perches and some rope perches made of natural fibers, such as hemp or

Your parrot's home

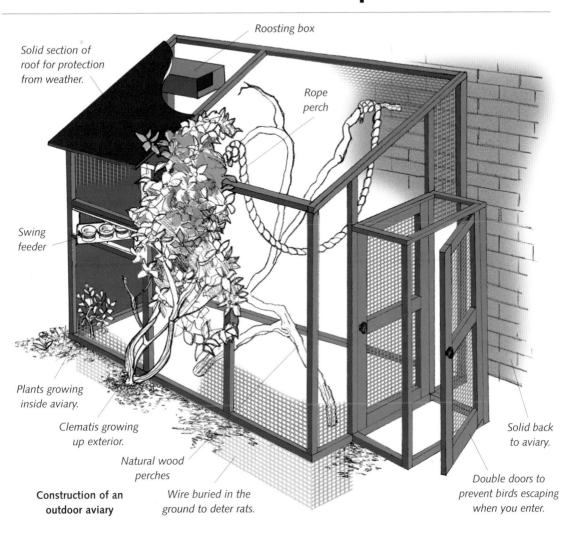

Solid section of roof for protection from weather.

Roosting box

Rope perch

Swing feeder

Plants growing inside aviary.

Clematis growing up exterior.

Natural wood perches

Construction of an outdoor aviary

Wire buried in the ground to deter rats.

Solid back to aviary.

Double doors to prevent birds escaping when you enter.

cotton. Many parrot aviaries are still poorly equipped. Despite what you may have heard, provided your aviary is large enough you can

Left: *Clematis is an ideal plant to grow over part of the aviary to provide some shade.*

usually get a range of plants to grow inside it. Again, this natural backdrop helps the birds feel more at home and relaxed. Make sure you have some toys and large food and water bowls as well. When taking your bird out to the aviary, always assume (even if it is wing-clipped) that it could fly off. Use a traveling cage and take it into the aviary where you can then release the bird.

A healthy diet

Parrots require a healthy balanced diet that comprises a range of different types of foods. The usual sunflower-seed-based pet parrot foods are totally unsuitable as the main constituent of a parrot's diet, as these are far too high in fat and lacking in important vitamins and minerals. The quality of seeds supplied to the pet food trade varies greatly. To determine seed quality, you can do a simple germination test. Pick out 100 of the seeds at random and soak them for 24 hours in

Above: *As this cockatoo flies many miles each day in the wild, it needs far more food than the same species living as a companion bird in the home.*

plain water at room temperature. Then drain the water off and keep them moist for another four or five days. Count how many of the seeds have germinated. Good seeds will have a small shoot growing out within four or five days, and you should expect about 90 percent to germinate like this. Any seeds that do not germinate may be dead, rancid or moldy, and these can pose a

serious threat to your bird's health if eaten. Many bird vets state that a bad seed-based diet is the most common cause of medical problems in pet parrots. Parrots are also often wrongly given even more fatty foods as treats—cookies, cheese, even meat. Such a diet can cause a bird to be chronically sick, typically with liver and kidney disorders.

LIKES VERSUS NEEDS

Parrots are, however, programmed to eat foods that are high in either fats or sugars and will try to eat these in preference to other foods. These foods give the bird the most calories for the minimum of effort. Their liking for these foods is natural, since in the wild they need lots of high-energy, high-fat food as fuel for flying hundreds of miles each week between feeding sites. However, in captivity parrots do not need such a high intake of rich food, since they will only fly relatively short distances around your home and cannot burn off the excess calories. So, for pet parrots the best diet should be mainly carbohydrate (about 75–80 percent) with around 15 percent vegetable protein and only 5–8 percent fat. Many bird food manufacturers still fail to list details of the amounts of fat, protein and carbohydrate on their food packets, but human foods are properly labeled and of better quality than the same items sold as pet foods.

To find the nutritional content of what you are giving your bird, you can always check the label on the same type of food that is sold for human consumption in a supermarket. Typical fat content of these is: 48 percent for sunflower seeds, 68 percent for pine nuts and 50 percent for peanuts. Conversely, legumes such as peas and beans have little or no fat and contain around 80 percent carbohydrate and 10–20 percent protein. Parrots do not have to have seeds available at all times, but soaked legumes, and fresh fruits and vegetables such as grapes, apples, bananas, carrots, celery, broccoli and pomegranates, should always be available. Nuts, which are very high in fat, should be fed sparingly.

Australian species, such as cockatoos, cockatiels and grass parakeets, can be fed drier foods including some dry seed. Cereal grains such as wheat, oats, millet, rice and maize are low in fats but high in carbohydrates and protein.

NUTRITIONAL VALUES OF SELECTED PARROT FOODS (per 5 oz./100 g of food)

	Type of food	Protein	Carbohydrates	Fat
	Mixed nuts: brazil nuts, almonds, hazelnuts, walnuts and pecans	¾ oz. 15.9 g	¼ oz. 4.9 g	3¼ oz. 64 g
	Mixed legumes: mung beans, green and brown lentils, aduki beans and chickpeas	⅞ oz. 16.8 g	2 oz. 43 g	⅙ oz. 3.1 g
	Raw peanuts (not roasted)	1¼ oz. 25.5 g	⅝ oz. 12.5 g	2⅓ oz. 46 g
	Chickpeas	1 oz. 21.4 g	2¼ oz. 45.2 g	¼ oz. 5.4 g
	Sunflower seeds	1 oz. 19.8 g	⁹⁄₁₀ oz. 18.6 g	2⅓ oz. 47.5 g

A healthy diet

If at present your bird's diet is mainly a parrot seed mixture, you should change its diet as it is deficient in several nutrients (see pages 92–93). There are two different types of healthier foods that you can offer your bird: either pelleted food or a fresh food mix of soaked and sprouted seeds and legumes with fresh fruit and vegetables. Pellets are usually nutritionally well balanced and some are organic. These foods are more convenient for the owner, particularly if you have lots of birds to feed. However, pellets may be very boring for your bird; a bit like you being forced to eat breakfast cereal for each and every meal! Pelleted food does not give the birds a chance to appreciate the different tastes and textures available to them in a more natural diet of seeds, fruit and vegetables.

A mixture of legumes (peas and beans) and some seeds can form the basis of most parrots' diets. Legumes are high in carbohydrate and protein with little or no fat. These pea and bean mixtures are best obtained as dry (human food)

Far left: *A mixture of dried legumes and seeds.*
Left: *The same mixture following soaking for 12 hours.*
Below left: *The same mixture after having sprouted and germinated, three days after soaking.*

mixtures from supermarkets. Legumes cannot be eaten as a dry food and have to be soaked and preferably sprouted (germinated) before being given to your bird.

When seeds are sprouted their vitamin content is increased. Regarding legumes, most parrots tend to like chickpeas best, but it's worth trying your bird on a mixture of different legumes at first to see which it prefers. The mixture can include chickpeas, mung beans, black-eyed peas, aduki beans and pinto beans. Once you know which beans your bird likes best, you can give more of these and less of the other kinds.

The following diet (which contains no dry seed at all) is recommended for most parrots:

35 percent soaked/sprouted beans or bean mix (chickpeas, black-eyed peas, mung beans, etc.).
25 percent soaked/sprouted seeds and cereal

Sunflower seeds   Chickpea   Soaked chickpea   Pine nut   Raisin   Sunflower seed   Melon seed

Your parrot's home

seeds and prevents them from germinating. It is quite normal for the beans to smell during this process. You can feed this soaked mixture after 12 hours, but rinse it thoroughly first in clean, cold water. However, a better option is to allow the mixture to sprout and germinate after another 12 to 24 hours. To do this, keep the food moist at room temperature but not soaking in water, and rinse it thoroughly several times in cold water to prevent any bacterial contamination of the food. When tiny white shoots appear on the seeds and beans, they are in the best condition to be given to your bird. Don't keep this food for more than one day after it is ready to eat; just throw away all leftovers. Don't cook any bean/seed mixes, nor keep them in a fridge; just feed it raw.

Above: *While pelleted foods are usually of good nutritional quality, they may be boring for your bird. Moistening pellets in plain, warm water can help to increase their acceptability.*

grains (sunflower, safflower, hemp, millet, wheat, oats, rice, maize, etc.).
40 percent fresh fruit and vegetables, such as apples, bananas, grapes, pomegranates, carrots, celery, sprouts, green beans, peas in the pod, sweet potato, corn on the cob, broccoli, etc.

PREPARING YOUR BIRD'S FOOD

You might find it easiest to first mix your legumes (35 percent of total food) and seed mixture (25 percent of total) together as a dry food. Daily amounts to give to birds will vary greatly between species and depend partly on how active the bird is. Rough examples are 1¾ ounces (50 g) dry weight for an African gray or Amazon, ⅞ ounce (25 g) dry weight for a cockatiel or Meyer's, 2¾ ounces (80 g) dry weight for a large macaw. On soaking, this amount will increase in weight as the seed absorbs water.

To prepare it, soak one day's amount in warm —but not hot—water for 12 hours, perhaps leaving it overnight as it cools. Hot water kills the

Right: *Vegetables tend to contain higher amounts of minerals than fruits, but they have a good vitamin content as well.*

A healthy diet

If your bird is eating a varied diet of fresh fruit, vegetables and legumes along with some seeds each day, there is little need for any other supplements. However, birds kept indoors will not have access to direct sunlight so they will not be able to make essential vitamin D_3. Without this, birds cannot convert calcium in their food for

Above: *It's easier to add supplements to a moist food, like this soaked seed and bean mix, than to dry foods.*

their bodily use, so your bird will need soluble calcium combined with vitamin D_3. This is available in liquid form from bird supplement suppliers.

The following foods are all harmful or toxic to birds and must be avoided: avocado (lethal), alcohol, chocolate, coffee and tea. All salty foods must be avoided as these can cause serious kidney problems. Beware of salt in human foods, including cheeses and breakfast cereals, and always read the nutrition information on the food packet. Birds cannot digest the fat (lactose) found

in milk, so the nutritional value of many dairy products is inaccessible to birds. However, parrots can digest fermented dairy products, such as yogurt and cheese, where the lactose has been broken down. But do take care regarding the salt content of these items and only feed small quantities. With only a few exceptions, parrots are not carnivorous and all meat should be avoided. Most cases of food poisoning (in humans and parrots) arise through infected meat, and cooking may not kill any viruses in meat that could then be acquired by your bird.

CHANGING YOUR BIRD'S DIET

This is really a behavioral issue, so the best way to change a bird's diet is first to ensure the bird is trained to accept basic requests from at least one person (see pages 60–83). Once this is done and the bird is bonded to you, you can introduce new foods by eating (or pretending to eat) them yourself in the presence of the bird. It is often best to do this with the bird away from its cage, perhaps when you are preparing the food first thing in the morning. Once the bird has eaten some of the new food while out of its cage, you can then try leaving some of it in the bird's food dishes, along with its usual food. You may have to do this for several days or even weeks, gradually increasing the quantity of the new food as you decrease the old. With birds that refuse to eat anything other than sunflower seed, try converting them at first to soaked and sprouted sunflower seed (see page 94). When the bird is eating this soaked seed withdraw all dry seed. Then, introduce soaked/sprouted legumes as well.

Your parrot's home

Above: *Hold any new food that you want to introduce up to your own mouth to get your bird interested in it. It helps if the new food is first offered warm.*

Below: *A good, varied diet is the key to a healthy bird, and all parrots appreciate a change from time to time.*

Another method, once the bird is beginning to accept a new food, is to feed this on its own as a first morning feed, then give a later feed of the old food in the afternoon. Gradually fade out the second feed as you increase the amount provided in the first feed. If you have several birds whose diets need changing, start with the most tame bird as it is likely to accept new things more quickly. The other birds are more likely to accept new foods when they see another bird already eating it.

Preventing & solving behavioral problems

WHAT CAUSES BEHAVIORAL PROBLEMS?

Do not try to dominate your bird by forcing it to do anything. Good behavior modification works by cooperating with your bird, not using forceful methods based on dominating it. The most common behavioral problems in parrots are nervousness, feather plucking, biting, excessive noise and destructive chewing behaviors. The causes of behavioral problems are many and varied, but the nature and quality of care that parrots receive as companion animals is at the heart of this issue. All animals have a behavioral repertoire, and they are hardwired to perform many behaviors on a daily basis if they are to be kept well both physically and mentally.

Animals such as dogs and horses have a behavioral need to run around and to socialize with other dogs or horses or people who understand them. Cats need some means of replicating their hunting behaviors; hamsters need to be able to make burrows in which to live. The range of behaviors is limitless and there are great variations between the many types of animals kept as pets. So long as most of these behaviors, or even just good substitutes for them, can be carried out, then the bird will have few problems. However, when a bird's attempts at carrying out its normal behaviors are frustrated, there is a serious

Above: *Wild hyacinth macaws. The natural habitat of parrots bears no resemblance to our living rooms.*

risk of behavioral problems arising.

Unlike domesticated pets, parrots, even captive-bred ones, remain essentially wild creatures with all their wild-type behaviors intact. The problem for parrots stems from the huge differences between the life they have evolved to live in their natural habitats and the life they are asked to live in our homes. The contrasts between these two living conditions are stark.

Right: *A bird in a barren cage will develop behavioral problems very rapidly and these can be hard to cure. Prevention by means of good quality care is the answer.*

COMPANIONSHIP IS VITAL

Most wild parrots live in large, highly social groups, flying hundreds of miles every week in their forest habitat. They will spend many hours each day finding foods from a range of sources. As highly intelligent creatures, they have a well-developed sense of play and spend much time playing with their flock mates. As preyed-upon creatures, vulnerable to attacks from many predators, they are highly nervous and suspicious in their behaviors. Indeed, their main protective measure is to live as a flock so that each bird can alert the others to any danger present. The very nature of the birds' social system—the highly integrated flock with its well-developed language of behavioral signals—gives the birds the security they need.

Contrast these conditions with those for the same bird transported to your living room. Here, typically, a parrot will live alone; there is no flock of birds. It will never fly any distance and may be confined to a cage for long periods. Food may be provided ad lib, with no requirement for it to search out different foods. The bird has time on its hands yet, often, absolutely nothing to do with all this time. A bird whose living conditions are so environmentally simplified is at great risk of

Above: *Yellow-naped Amazons use their climbing skills while feeding on ripening bananas in the trees of Honduras.*

Left: *Most parrots, like these scarlet macaws, form a close bond with their mate and mutual preening strengthens this relationship.*

being bored and frustrated. With birds as intelligent as parrots, it is vital to give them living conditions in which they can replicate as many of their natural, wild behaviors as possible.

Environmental enrichment

Preventing behavioral problems is of course easier than trying to correct things once they have gone wrong. Providing your bird with a stimulating environment with opportunities to exhibit as many natural behaviors as possible will greatly reduce the risk of behavioral problems arising.

Perhaps the most important aspect of a companion bird's care, particularly if you have only one bird, is the amount of time the bird spends out of the cage with you and your family. As highly social creatures, parrots cannot cope with solitude, so you and your family are your bird's substitute parrot flock. As long as your bird is trained and accepts requests as described in the Training Your Bird section, you should be able to have it out of the cage most of the time you are at home. Your bird will need to spend many hours, not just one or two hours, out of the cage with you each day. You should arrange for the bird to have several places it can go to in the rooms to which you allow it access. While parrots often like to have somewhere they can just crash out, they are liable to become frustrated if they are forced to stay in one place for too long. The use of parrot stands and several small tabletop stands is recommended.

Parrots that are in good mental health are highly inquisitive and will want to investigate things that interest them; provided it is safe, they should be allowed—indeed encouraged—to do this. It is important to keep the bird's beak and brain busy, both when it is in the cage and when the bird is out with you. Toys that can be held in the foot and preferably chewed to destruction

(left) will be of more interest to your bird than many other, often expensive, toys. Use your imagination to come up with ways in which the bird can forage for some favorite food treats. Cardboard tubes filled with newspaper in which some treats are hidden work very well. Pinecones spliced with peanut butter will be torn apart; hiding treats in small cardboard boxes presents more of a challenge.

MUTUAL PREENING IS ESSENTIAL

Wild parrots spend some time each day preening each other, and this behavior is necessary emotionally for them. You should replicate this behavior with your bird. This is best done by imitating the preening action of another bird, but confine your attention to your bird's head only. If you start to preen or touch it anywhere else the bird may become sexually overstimulated. Consequently, the bird may overbond to you and then become aggressive to other members of your family. The bird's cage should be of a large size with a range of perches, several toys (changed occasionally) and a roosting box. If you have a backyard consider having a day-flight for your bird's use during the daytime. Again, provide plenty of things for your bird to do in the aviary; branches to chew up, several toys to play with and perhaps another roosting box. If you are considering getting a second bird as a companion for your first bird, the two may pair up. When this happens, your bird may not want to have anything to do with you and may even become aggressive toward you or other people.

Preventing & solving behavioral problems

TOILET TRAINING AND CHEWING

When you let birds roam loose around the house, inevitably you must expect them to create droppings outside their cage and perhaps chew on wooden items in the home. Some people do train their birds to void on command, often when being asked to come out of the cage. To teach this, you ask the bird to "step up" onto your hand from the cage, take him out and put it down in a place where you want it to perform. If it voids within a short time, you reward it with something that you know it likes. Then you take it up from its voiding perch and interact with it as usual. If you wish to avoid droppings

on furniture, you need to be attuned to your bird's ways and anticipate when next it will need to go, at which time you return it either to its cage or its voiding perch. This approach can sometimes cause some birds problems, as they (or their owners) become obsessed with only passing droppings in certain places. You need to be careful about this training.

Alternatively, most owners are relatively relaxed about this. You can position tissue or a newspaper beneath your bird's favorite perching places or just clean up after it with a tissue.

Some parrots try to chew anything they can get their beaks into, including your furniture. When someone reacts to a bird's chewing by saying "No," the chewing behavior is likely to become more frequent, since the bird perceives that it is being rewarded with attention. The best solution is to provide the bird with alternative items to chew on and encourage it to do so by rewarding this behaviour with attention. The best items to use as chewing toys are those made from natural materials, such as corks (left), clothes pegs, pinecones (below), small pieces of rolled-up newspaper, or short lengths of natural fiber rope or cord.

Nervous & phobic parrots

Typically, a bird that is said to be phobic is one that has previously been tame, even confident in its behavior, but has suddenly developed a fear of a person, object or action. This is a learned condition; something has happened to the bird to cause it to have a strong fear reaction to some particular stimulus. Often, birds develop a sudden fear of a particular object or action or even the close approach of their own carer. Birds that can't fly are more vulnerable to this condition since they will also have a frustrated escape reflex action, which exacerbates their fear stimulus. This means the bird is aware that it cannot fly away from any perceived problem.

Anything that may be interpreted by the bird as a predator or is associated with pain is likely to cause a panic reaction. Objects that might seem utterly harmless to us can have this

Left: A parrot may find someone looking like this very frightening because of the similarity to a predator's staring gaze.

effect. A carrier bag, dark-colored cloth or clothing, or people wearing hats can cause great fear in a bird. If the bird cannot escape a fearful stimulus because it is caged and/or wing-clipped, then a severe panic attack can occur. Every tiny detail of any fearful event or object will be remembered by the bird, and should a similar frightening event recur, the bird's panic reaction will be repeated.

PROTECT FROM FEAR
Another common cause of phobic behavior is the carer's response to a bird when it is in some

Below and below left: When a bird has crash-landed do not approach it immediately. Always wait until it has collected its senses before asking it to step up.

Preventing & solving behavioral problems

difficulty. If a bird crashes into a window or falls to the floor dazed and confused and the carer immediately approaches to help it, the bird will associate this close approach with the cause of the accident and any pain it is suffering. The carer's face, hands and perhaps any clothing he or she might be wearing will be associated with the problem. When the bird sees these things again, its fear response will be triggered and it may have a phobic panic attack again. The only way to help a bird in these situations is simply to remove yourself from the bird's view until it has had a few minutes to compose itself.

Wherever possible, make sure a bird is never exposed to other fearful objects or actions. If it reacts to someone wearing a hat, then no one should approach your bird with a hat on. If this cannot be done, perhaps because the bird sees

Left: *A bird that has developed a phobic reaction may be fearful of its carer's hands because they are associated with the event that caused its original panic attack.*

you or your hands as part of the problem, a careful process of desensitizing the bird to the problem can be carried out. However, it is vital that this is done at a pace that the bird finds acceptable. In the case of the bird being fearful of you, you will need to work on a program where you gradually reteach your bird to accept your close approach. Here, you will need to use the techniques explained on pages 62–63 for nervous birds, where you gradually ask your bird to allow you to make a closer approach each day. Again, birds that have not been wing-clipped will tend to make better progress than clipped birds.

Self-plucking

It is very distressing for both the parrot and its carer when a bird starts to damage its own feathers. Scientific studies have shown that the problem is caused by frustration and overuse of the cage. As with any behavior, self-plucking is done by the bird because it perceives some benefit from it. Self-plucking is a form of self-harm that can sometimes lead to self-mutilation of the skin. The condition usually starts with a bird tearing, rather than actually removing, some of its feathers. Later, the bird may try to pull its feathers out, usually removing its body feathers or the underlying down feathers. Feather plucking is a problem only for captive birds; wild parrots do not feather pluck or self-mutilate, so the causes are certainly due to conditions in captivity.

Left: *This galah self-mutilates its back and has a flesh wound there. The collar and disk stop the problem, but this is not a cure.*

really is an illness of the pet parrot kept in a cage without the company of other birds or the ability to perform its natural behaviors. Providing good environmental enrichment (see page 100) and ensuring that your bird spends many hours each day out of the cage, able to fly, all help to prevent self-plucking.

If a bird is self-plucking it is vital to act promptly in order to have a much better chance of curing the problem. While all plucking has a behavioral component (it is a voluntary behavior), the bird should be seen by a specialist avian vet to determine its true state of health. Some

VULNERABLE BIRDS

Certain species (and practices) make some parrots far more likely to pluck than others. African grays, cockatoos and macaws seem the most vulnerable species. Parrots that have been hand-reared from the egg, and therefore deprived of their natural parents, may be more vulnerable to self-plucking than parent-reared birds. Hand-reared birds are also very prone to overbonding to one person (see page 37). Parrots that have been wing-clipped, especially clipped as an immature bird, or birds that spend too long each day in a cage are also very vulnerable to plucking. In contrast, birds kept with other parrots in large naturalistic aviaries rarely self-pluck. Plucking

Above and right: *This citron-crested cockatoo was cage bound and very unhappy. She suffers from stereotypical behaviors and also damages her head feathers with her feet. Most of the crest is also missing.*

Preventing & solving behavioral problems

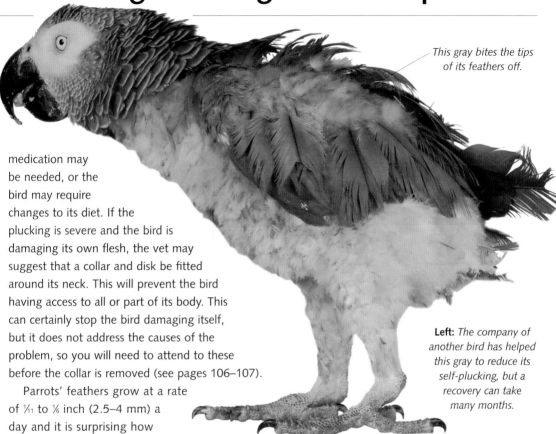

This gray bites the tips of its feathers off.

medication may be needed, or the bird may require changes to its diet. If the plucking is severe and the bird is damaging its own flesh, the vet may suggest that a collar and disk be fitted around its neck. This will prevent the bird having access to all or part of its body. This can certainly stop the bird damaging itself, but it does not address the causes of the problem, so you will need to attend to these before the collar is removed (see pages 106–107).

Parrots' feathers grow at a rate of ⅟₁₁ to ⅙ inch (2.5–4 mm) a day and it is surprising how

Left: *The company of another bird has helped this gray to reduce its self-plucking, but a recovery can take many months.*

quickly the body feathers can come back. Often within two weeks you will see good regrowth. The situation with wing feathers is different. If the bird has damaged wing feather stumps remaining, these will not regrow until the bird molts them out naturally (see page 111). However, a good bird vet can either repair these feathers by attaching donor feathers, or immediate feather regrowth can be induced by removing the feather stumps while the bird is anesthetized. The new feathers will grow back immediately at the same rate of growth, but such large feathers take several weeks to be fully grown.

Self-plucking

It is certainly far easier to resolve any behavioral problem if the bird is already tame and confident in the presence of its carer. If this is not the case, the bird should be trained so that it can be handled easily and is reasonably confident in the presence of its carers. Just follow the methods outlined in the Training Your Bird section. Self-plucking is often unintentionally reinforced by the bird's carer. If a bird plucks and is then reprimanded by its carer who says "No" or "Stop that," the bird may see this as receiving attention for plucking. Such behavior by the bird's carer may encourage the plucking. Any form of reinforcement, including such unintended reinforcement, must be avoided.

If a bird is already spending most of the day out of the cage and plucks in the company of people, the best action to take is to leave the room every time the bird damages its feathers. You may have to repeat this many times, but once a bird that is bonded to you realizes that its plucking is causing you to leave, it then has an incentive to cease plucking. A bird should never be returned to its cage for any unwanted behavior as this can make matters even worse. The use of the cage as a form of punishment is

Above: *Self-plucking often starts with damage being done to feathers on the legs.*

Left: *Moluccan cockatoos are very vulnerable to self-plucking. These social and intelligent birds become bored and frustrated very easily if they are kept caged for too long.*

counterproductive. When you start to react by walking out on your bird when it plucks in your company, you need to be consistent about it. Often with this method the plucking initially gets worse as the bird tests the new tactic you are employing. This very temporary increase in an unwanted behavior is called extinction burst. It is a precursor to the cessation of the behavior, so it tells you the bird is learning!

KEEP THE BIRD OCCUPIED

Some birds self-pluck while out of the cage but only in certain locations. Here, the behavior is location specific. In these cases the simple solution is to deny the bird access to those places that might cause it to pluck.

Preventing & solving behavioral problems

When a bird plucks when no one is with it, perhaps during the night, then there is little you can do by direct behavior modification. In such cases you will need to review all of the bird's living conditions. Does the bird enjoy many hours each day out of the cage? Does it interact with you or with other birds and play with toys? Are you providing the bird with opportunities to forage for some of its favorite foods and to chew up toys? The more opportunities you can give your bird to replicate as many of its wild-type natural behaviors, the more likely you are to reduce the plucking

behavior. Included among these activities are daily periods during which your bird can fly. The use of an outdoor day-flight aviary will also be of benefit, but this needs to be a place that is interesting and stimulating for your bird, as well as somewhere the bird feels safe. It should be fitted with a range of perches, branches to chew and toys, and offer means of encouraging your bird to search for foods. To encourage good feather condition, parrots should be sprayed at least every other day with plain water. Use a plant sprayer for this, set to spray your bird gently with a fine mist of water droplets.

Above: *When spraying your parrot with water to improve feather condition, spray upward from below the level at which the bird is sitting and let the water droplets fall down gently onto it.*

Left: *Dry feathers will break and fray and irritate the bird. If your bird is not used to being sprayed, start with very brief showers, then, on subsequent days, increase the shower sessions until you can get the bird thoroughly wet. In the wild they get drenched most days.*

Wing-clipping

Parrots are often clipped because their owners feel this is needed to control their bird and that it is easier to manage a clipped bird. Some say it is safer for the bird. However, if you implement the basic training described in this book, including teaching your bird to accept some flight requests, you can have good control over your bird's flying activities. Other parrot-care books often assume that parrots should be clipped, but here you will find details of how to keep your bird full winged rather than clipped.

Convex surface above wing

Air flow *Low pressure*

Air flow

Air flow

High pressure

LIFT *LIFT*

Concave surface below wing

Air flow

Air flow

Above: *Birds use their wings to lever themselves through the air. This Timneh gray is half-way through its downstroke. Note the twisted primaries as they force air backward to propel the bird forward.*

DIFFERENT TYPES OF WING-CLIP

Clipping involves shortening the bird's main flight feathers (the primary feathers). Sometimes this is done to one wing only. This deliberately unbalances the bird if it attempts to fly and is the worst kind of clipping. Other forms of clipping are less crude, where both wings are clipped evenly but lightly to allow the bird to fly down and land safely while indoors.

PROBLEMS WITH WING-CLIPPING

Both clipped and full-winged birds are subject to some dangers; clipped birds are just subject to different risks than normal full-winged birds. If severely clipped birds escape from the home, they are vulnerable to predation by cats, dogs, hawks or being run down by a car. Clipped birds have little control with regard to braking in flight but will still attempt to fly if something startles them. These birds are at risk of crash landing and injuring themselves badly. For a bird to be clipped

yet still able to recover from a fall and land safely indoors (in still air), the type of clip must be quite mild and be equal on both wings. However, if such a mildly clipped bird escapes in even a light breeze it will be able to gain height and fly quite well, since moving air generates more lift for the bird than the still, dead air indoors. Conversely, if the bird is clipped so severely that it cannot possibly take flight outdoors, the severity of such a clip threatens the safety of the bird due to crash landings on hard surfaces.

Flight is a parrot's prime means of ensuring its own safety. When a bird feels frightened, it has an instinctive reflex action to take flight immediately to escape from the source of danger. Once away from the hazard, the bird's fear will subside. The most serious aspect of wing-clipping is that it denies a bird this most vital predator-avoidance response, and the frustration of this fundamental behavior can cause severe behavioral problems for

Preventing & solving behavioral problems

Below: *Right wing of a Meyer's parrot. This bird is molting. It has only nine of its ten primary feathers. Number 9 primary, near the outer end, is only part-grown. The feather will be fully grown within four days and will then be the longest flight feather.*

Bottom: *This shows how some people might wing-clip a bird such as this Meyer's parrot by cutting its primary feathers. Such a clip seriously compromises the safety of the bird.*

Above: *The only reason this gray's tail is so clearly visible is because both its wings have been severely clipped.*

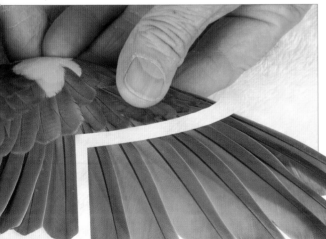

parrots. Furthermore, clipping any immature bird (under 2 years old) can impair the normal development of the bird's heart and wing muscles and affect it for the rest of its life. Young birds have a strong urge to fly, but flying skills have to be learned, so these birds are clumsy while learning. This clumsiness is quite normal but, on seeing it, some people think the bird would be safer if it was clipped. But clipping at this stage would be disastrous for the bird as it will still try to fly, but now it will have no means to control itself and is at even greater risk of injury. If left to learn to fly, the bird will soon acquire the skills it needs.

Repairing feathers

Parrots usually renew their flight feathers each year, but the larger macaws and cockatoos may retain flight feathers for up to two years before molting. Molting allows a bird to regrow any clipped feathers, but a clipped bird remains vulnerable to damaging its new blood feathers as these grow down. These blood feathers need the protection of full-length neighboring feathers to avoid being damaged. Bleeding from broken blood feathers can be profuse and painful. Most parrots have nine or ten primary feathers that are attached to the "hand." The primaries provide propulsion during take off, are used as brakes with a reverse thrust action on landing and (with the tail) help in steering. They are numbered P1 to P10 (see illustration opposite). Parrots also have 12 secondary flight feathers along the "forearm." The airfoil shape of these feathers provides free lift as air passes over them. The bird's main wing and tail feathers grow at ¹⁄₁₀ to ⅙ inch (3 – 4 mm) per day. A typical 6 inch (150 mm) long primary feather in a gray or Amazon will take about 40 days to grow down. The bird may molt two, sometimes three, flight feathers at a time on each wing.

Birds have evolved over millions of years as essentially flying creatures. As a consequence, birds have a much higher body temperature and higher heart and respiration rates than mammals. A flying bird's normal heartbeat can be over 1,000 beats per minute. As with any animal, birds need to be able to take regular, vigorous exercise to be healthy, and the exercise needs to be sufficiently vigorous to raise the rate of heartbeat significantly. This can only be achieved by daily periods of flight. Flying birds are much stronger than clipped ones and tend to have more resistance to illnesses than non-flying birds.

REPAIRING CLIPPED WINGS

If a bird has been clipped, it is best to have the wings repaired without delay. This is particularly important with immature birds. Young parrots have a behavioral window within the first few months of life in which they acquire flying skills, and this should be encouraged, even though they will be clumsy as they learn to fly. If they fail to learn to fly properly during this period, they may never learn to fly well at all. Avian vets can restore flight in clipped birds or those with damaged flight feathers in two ways. Donor feathers from the same species can be splinted (imped) back on, or the damaged feathers can be removed under anesthetic and regrowth will commence immediately. Waiting for a bird to regrow its feathers by molting, rather than imping or pulling, will still mean that the bird is denied flight for up to a year. During this time there is also

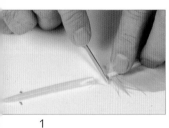

1

2

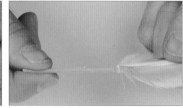

3

4

Preventing & solving behavioral problems

THE MOLTING SEQUENCE

In a normal, healthy parrot starting to molt, the first feather to be dropped and replaced will be a central primary, usually P6. As the primary feathers are being molted and replaced, this process continues in both directions of the primary web simultaneously, so the whole sequence is: P6, P5 and P7, P4 and P8, P3 and P9, P2 and P10, P1. Once this sequence is well underway, the bird will then start to molt and replace its secondaries. Here, the sequence is simply linear. S1 is the first secondary to be lost and replaced and S12 the last. In a normal molting sequence a healthy parrot will molt the same feathers on each wing at the same time; this ensures they remain perfectly symmetrical. A parrot should never be missing more than three flight feathers from either wing at any time. Parrots have 12 tail feathers, and again these are molted in an even pattern with the central two feathers being molted and replaced first, and the outer two being renewed last.

P6   S1

10 primaries   12 secondaries   First secondary to be molted.   First primary to be molted.

L6   L1 R1   R6

First pair of tail feathers to be molted.

a risk of the bird damaging its blood feathers as they grow down.

As flight is such an important part of a bird's normal behavioral repertoire, it should always be encouraged and not denied them. By including the flight requests as part of any companion bird's normal training regime, it is not difficult to keep your bird without clipping its wings.

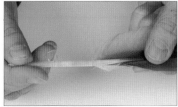

5

Far left to left: *Preparing a feather for imping onto a clipped bird's wing. **1.** A donor feather has part of its shaft removed. **2.** A small bamboo splint is prepared. **3. and 4.** Half of the splint is inserted and glued into the hollow shaft of the donor feather. **5.** The donor feather is then ready to be used by splinting it onto the stump of a feather on the bird's clipped wing.*

Aggression & biting

Before trying to solve any biting problem, the bird will need to be trained to accept the usual requests from you. If a bird bites during training, it is best to train it to step on and off a stick-perch (see page 68) instead of your hand, as this reduces the risk of being bitten. Most people who keep parrots are bitten occasionally, but most biting is usually not hard enough to cause real pain.

Above: *Parrots are not naturally aggressive birds. But if upset or provoked, they can bite hard.*

If you are bitten regularly or hard, the problem needs to be resolved. Such biting can be caused by the bird being nervous, angry, overexcited or frightened. If a bird is overbonded to one person, it may bite other people as a form of jealousy biting. Also, young birds often don't realize the strength of their own beaks and have to learn what degree of biting is acceptable. Some birds are aware that some people are nervous of the beak; such birds may bite to test the person's reaction.

ALWAYS STAY CALM

However, one of the most common reasons for a hard bite is that the bird has become overexcited, perhaps while you are playing with it. Here, it is not the bird's fault. Just make sure to prevent such overexcitement during play sessions. If you are bitten at these times, try to show as little reaction as you can and avoid saying anything. Just grit your teeth, accept that a mistake has been made and remove your hands from the bird as calmly as you can for a few minutes. Remain calm until the bird also calms down. On no account should a bird that has bitten be returned to its cage. If you do this, the next problem you will have is that the bird will be difficult to put back in the cage on later occasions! A much more effective and appropriate reaction to being bitten is to calmly remove yourself from the company of your bird. Just turn your back on the bird, walk out of the room and close the door behind you, leaving the

Above: *It is best to avoid direct eye contact when a bird lands on your shoulder.*

Preventing & solving behavioral problems

Once the bird realizes that its antisocial behavior has caused you to leave, it will have the incentive to cease biting. Remember, saying anything—especially "No!" in a loud voice—or wagging your finger in front of the bird will only make things much worse, since the bird will become more excited and its behavior more uninhibited and more aggressive. Biting can also be associated with particular places. If this is the case (outside of the cage), the

Above: *A bird is never at fault when it bites its carer since it is not in control of its living conditions.*

bird wherever it happens to be. Stay out of the room for a few minutes only. When you return, make sure both you and the bird are calm before you try to interact with one another, then carry on as normal. When it step ups, praise it enthusiastically. If the bird bites hard again, be consistent and again calmly walk out of the room.

bird should be denied access to these places for some time. Birds that are allowed to remain on the shoulder will often eventually bite. The shoulder may be used as a landing place as the bird flies to you. But as soon as it lands there, give the "step up" request and transfer it to your hand. Always turn your head away from the bird as you do this to avoid looking at it.

Above: *Offer your hand and calmly give the "step up" request; keep your thumb down.*

Above: *Bring the bird down slowly and praise it for its cooperation after it has stepped up.*

Screaming

It is quite usual for parrots to make a lot of loud noise as part of their normal behavior. Periods of normal high-volume calls are usually of limited duration (less than one hour) and occur during the early morning and again in the evening.

Above: *The size of a bird is no measure of the volume of its call! The ring-necked parakeet is fairly small but has a very loud contact call.*

Abnormal repetitive, continuous screaming will be caused by some other underlying problem, usually boredom, frustration or anxiety. It starts with overuse of a contact call as the bird asks for the attention of its carer. This is common with many cockatoos, which scream when their carer leaves the room and the bird is left alone. Shouting at the bird, or even covering the cage, are unlikely to address the causes of screaming. Returning a screaming bird to its cage is often counterproductive.

SIGNS OF FRUSTRATION

Birds may also scream when they can see you doing something, perhaps eating, from within their cage and are frustrated because they cannot join in with you. If the bird cannot come out of the cage to join you, you should eat out of sight of the bird.

The methods below have proved useful in reducing screaming in parrots where the bird appears to be making noise for attention and wants to keep in contact with you when you leave the room. You could try these methods with your bird but only if:

- the bird's screaming is genuinely excessive;
- the bird is already trained and accepts the usual requests from you;
- it is already getting several hours a day out of the cage with you.

First, teach the bird to recognize the difference between times when you leave the room briefly while remaining within earshot of the bird and other times when you leave the room for a long period, perhaps when leaving the house. When leaving the bird just to go briefly to another room before returning, leave the door ajar and use a contact call that is quieter than the bird's screaming call, such as a soft whistle or just the bird's name. The bird should learn to listen for your contact call, and it can only do this when it is not calling itself. So keep in vocal contact with your bird while you are nearby but out of sight of it. When first teaching this, just leave the room for a few seconds only. Then gradually work up to leaving for a few minutes.

When leaving for a longer period ensure the bird is in its cage but close the room door and tell

Preventing & solving behavioral problems

Right: *Gray parrots are not usually known to be loud birds, but they will sometimes imitate any loud noise if it is repeated frequently in their company.*

the bird you will be gone some time. Do not return for more than 30 minutes. Some birds learn the difference between these two types of disappearance of their carers and screaming is reduced. You should, of course, always encourage other activities that are behaviorally incompatible with screaming, such as playing with (and tearing apart) destructible toys and use of a roosting box for a daytime siesta. Birds will not scream when inside their roosting box.

If the bird screams excessively while you are in the same room, just leave the room, closing the door behind you. Do not return for at least 10 minutes and do not answer any contact call the bird gives. You may have to do this many times before the bird realizes that its screaming causes you to leave the room.

Above left to right: *Busy beaks don't scream! Keeping your bird occupied with a range of different tasks will reduce boredom. This gray's puzzle toy has different-sized holes. Larger food items can only be extracted from one hole. This behavior replicates some feeding methods the bird would use in the wild.*

Destructive behaviors

Parrots are naturally messy birds and need to be able to chew things to destruction. This is part of their normal behavior; in the wild it is associated with nesting and feeding activities. If they are not provided with suitable items to chew, they may chew on your furniture, doors or other objects instead. All parrots should be given opportunities to chew on acceptable materials. These can be its toys, perches, branches, the roosting box and anything inside the box. Birds should also be provided with items outside the cage to chew on. Any chewable toys made out of natural (not plastic)

Above: *The urge to chew is very strong in many parrots. If birds are not given opportunities to chew on legitimate items, they may direct their attention onto anything they can find, including doors and picture frames.*

materials—such as rope, natural untreated wood, corks, clothes pegs, untreated leather, cardboard, paper, including old phone books—are suitable. When introducing any new items to your bird, make sure that it sees you playing with them first as this will give it more confidence to investigate and use the new toys.

ONE-PERSON BIRDS

Birds that have been hand-reared rather than parent-reared are far more likely to overbond to one person. Usually, this manifests itself by the bird behaving as though its favored person were its sexual partner. If the bird is no longer immature, it may also be

Left: *This gray has a ring made of many layers of cardboard. Often, such chewing toys are irresistible and birds love to tear them apart.*

Preventing & solving behavioral problems

aggressive to other people or pets in the same room. The instinctive urges that cause this can be so strong that behavior modification is not easy to carry out. It is easier to avoid overbonding by not having a hand-reared bird in the first place. However, to reduce the chances of this behavior in a hand-reared bird, you should ensure you do not interact with it such that it gets sexually excited. Avoid touching the bird anywhere other than on its head, where you can offer head scratches as you imitate the preening action of another bird. Even then, make sure to keep such head scratching to a few brief seconds only. Have other members of your family work one on one with the bird in basic training sessions. If the problem cannot be fully overcome and the bird is aggressive, make sure other family members use the "stay" request to stop the bird from approaching them.

BAD LANGUAGE

Parrots are inclined to imitate loud sounds associated with dramatic actions, including people gesticulating. This is why they often pick up swear words. Obviously it's best to avoid swearing in front of your bird! However, to affect a cure you will need to make absolutely sure you do not unintentionally reinforce your bird's swearing when it does occur. In such a case, say absolutely nothing. A more effective reaction is to remove yourself from the bird's company for a few minutes each time it swears. If the bird likes you (through the basic training it should have received), it will eventually cease swearing. But if it does not like you, it may not cease!

FREE-RANGE BIRDS

Free-range birds are those that are out of their cages at all times but not provided with any training or supervision while out; the birds are left to do their own thing. While immature birds may be kept this way briefly, without formal training, as soon as the bird matures you are likely to encounter behavioral problems as the bird becomes more aggressive. It is important to ensure that your bird is trained to accept the requests described earlier, especially the flight requests, and that you keep up with this requirement. Untrained birds often become aggressive by default, but this is easy to avoid with training.

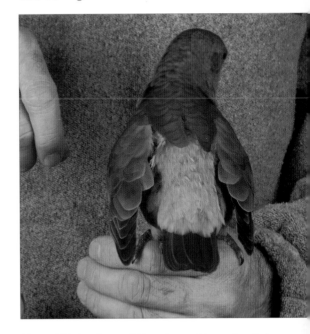

Above: *This hand-reared Meyer's parrot is overbonded to its main carer. The bird's dropped wings and exposed rump show it is sexually aroused.*

Escaped parrots

It is quite common for parrots to escape. Most escape through an open door or window. Many "shoulder birds" are lost when the bird's carer walks outdoors forgetting about the bird on their

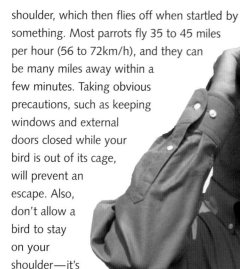

Above: *Countless birds escape, particularly in the summer, when someone forgets about the bird on their shoulder as they walk out the door.*

shoulder, which then flies off when startled by something. Most parrots fly 35 to 45 miles per hour (56 to 72km/h), and they can be many miles away within a few minutes. Taking obvious precautions, such as keeping windows and external doors closed while your bird is out of its cage, will prevent an escape. Also, don't allow a bird to stay on your shoulder—it's

all too easy to forget that it is there, and it may be too late if you then walk outside.

However, in the event of an escape, you should have these items ready:

- a good pair of binoculars;
- some of your bird's favorite food treats and the food bowl from the cage;
- a traveling case and/or cloth bag with drawstrings to put the bird in if you do catch it.

Birds behave differently depending on the nature of the escape. If a bird panicked while escaping, it will probably fly a great distance before coming down to land in an exhausted state. However, a bird that escapes while otherwise quite calm usually does not go far. Indeed, in this case the bird is most likely to fly in a wide circle around the point of escape, looking for somewhere to land. For most parrots who find themselves flying outdoors, the whole world is a very confusing place because the bird will not be familiar with what it sees. Parrots do not like to land on any perch unless they are already familiar with it. Tree branches, which could be blowing in the wind, may be frightening to such a bird, and bare rooftops may also not be acceptable. It is this unfamiliarity

Left: *A good pair of binoculars (x8 magnification recommended) are invaluable in searching for a lost parrot.*

CHAPTER 10

Left: *Once in unfamiliar conditions outdoors, a bird will be confused and may fly several miles away.*

use your usual calls and whistles as you search for your bird.

It's worth making copies of a short note with a picture of your bird and dropping this into as many homes as you can in your neighborhood. This should have details of the date and time you lost the bird and all your contact details. When someone

with the outdoors that often confuses a bird and forces it to fly until it has to land through sheer exhaustion.

finds a strange bird or just sees it in their garden, they often contact the police, local radio station, local veterinary practice or local animal shelter. You should also contact these organizations with details of your lost bird.

SPREAD THE WORD

When it does land, initially it will be very tense and liable to take flight again unless given time to calm down. Often birds select to land on the tallest tree in the area, and then they try to hide from view by climbing down into the foliage, remaining hidden. In winter, when most trees have lost their leaves, it is easier to find a bird by direct searching using your binoculars. However, in summer it can be extremely difficult to spot a parrot in a tree. In this case it's best to rely on your ears to start with, listening for your bird's calls. Companion birds (as opposed to most aviary birds) will often respond to the familiar voice of their carer, so

Above: *After an escaped bird has landed in a tree, it will often take cover and hide in the foliage.*

Recovering a lost bird

When you do find your bird, it may be high up in a tree or on a roof, and most birds will not fly down to you, even if you are offering food. The bird's instincts tell it to stay high up, where it will feel much safer. However, a bird will often try to walk to you if you can approach it in a way that offers it a route that doesn't require it to fly. Usually this means that you have to get a ladder and make some attempt to go up to your bird. Even if you are only a few feet off the ground with your ladder against the tree, the bird will often start climbing down to you. At this point, be sure to have some of your bird's favorite food ready. With most birds, it is best to offer them a small tidbit and stay with the bird as it eats this to calm it down.

At some point, depending on how the bird is used to being handled, you will have to decide how you are going to secure it. Birds trained to accept the usual requests will still obey all of them outdoors. A trained bird is very likely to "step up" when asked to and just walk onto your hand. If you are up a tree, you should have a soft cloth bag into which you can put the bird before you climb down, but do not let the

Left: Escaped birds often lack the confidence to fly down from their perch in the treetops, even if they recognize you.

bird see this until you have secured it. You can make a suitable bag from a small pillowcase. It should have a drawstring and a strap that goes over your shoulder to leave your hands free. Or you can carefully lower the bag down to the ground on a long line.

If you find your bird but are not able to catch it by nightfall, return to the same place before light the next morning and try again. Most parrots do not fly after dark, so your bird should still be there.

IF YOUR BIRD IS NOT TAME

Birds that are not hand tame are more difficult to recover and require different techniques. If you have another similar bird, you can try putting it in a cage and place another cage alongside it containing food to attract the bird down. You'll need to devise a way of closing the cage door from a suitable distance. The decoy and trap cages both need to be reasonably high up off the ground to tempt an escaped bird down.

Escaped parrots that find food quickly, behave normally and fly confidently will

Left: Place your bird in a bag with drawstrings and a shoulder strap when you recover it from up a tree. This leaves your hands free and allows you to climb down safely.

Escaped parrots

a month at liberty, so keep up your efforts to find your bird. The more people you tell about your bird, and the more people you can persuade to help you, the better your chances of getting your bird back.

Left: *This escaped Timneh gray seems quite at home eating ripe rowan berries from a tree.*
Below: *By making some effort to go up to your bird, you stand more chance of it climbing down through the branches to meet you.*

usually have few problems with their freedom, except in times of prolonged cold weather. Most native wild birds will leave parrots alone, provided they appear confident in their behaviors. Once an escaped parrot has found a good source of food, it is very likely to remain in that area for several days at least. Parrots are intelligent birds and soon learn to come to bird tables and bird feeders for food or take fruits from garden shrubs. Any bird that survives the first three days outdoors has a good chance of long-term survival in temperate climates. Some birds are recovered after well over

First aid

Left: *Check the condition of the bird's vent regularly: this should be clean and not fouled with the remains of any droppings.*

With a good, varied diet, daily periods of exercise, a stimulating environment and a good relationship with its carer, your bird should stay both physically and mentally healthy. However, you should always be prepared for the possibility of illness. For proper treatment of your bird, you will need the services of a vet who specializes in birds. Vets who are good with dogs and cats may not be competent with birds, and the treatment they offer may cause further problems. Vets who are experienced in the care of parrots are not as widespread as regular small animal vets, so don't assume that you will find a suitable vet close to you. Avian vets are listed each month in *Parrots* magazine and on parrot-related websites. These vets will have some or all of the following facilities:

- anesthesia by isoflourane gas (this is a very safe form of anesthesia for birds);
- ability to do imping (restoring flight by repairing a bird's wing feathers);
- ability to do complete blood count and biochemistry tests;
- use of an endoscope for internal examinations;
- ability to take tissue samples (biopsies) for testing;
- staff who understand how to handle parrots correctly and confidently, using a towel (not gloves) to minimize stress;
- 24-hour hospitalization facilities for birds.

Healthy birds are active for most, but not all, of the daytime. The eyes should be bright and wide open. There should be no discharge from the nostrils and the breathing should be silent. The bird should be alert and well aware of things going on around it. The body feathers should be relaxed and slightly smoothed down, neither puffed up nor lying down on the body with an excessive tightness. The bird should be eating its food normally and passing droppings normally, without undue straining. The area around the vent should be clean, not soiled by droppings. When resting or sleeping, a healthy bird usually stands on one foot. If your bird does not show these normal healthy signs, something may be wrong. Remember, sick birds will always try to hide signs of illness until no longer capable of doing so.

ACT WITHOUT DELAY

Sick birds often appear tired, with fluffed up feathers and sunken, dull or half-closed eyes. They may have difficulty using a perch or with balancing and may go to the floor of the cage. A sick bird often shows signs of being less aware of things going on around it. The droppings may not be normal, and the bird may not be eating as usual. Sick birds often lose weight quickly. Make sure you know your bird's normal weight and check this from time to time. If the bird appears ill

Right: *Use good kitchen scales and make sure that you know your bird's normal, healthy weight. Tell the vet if this changes when your bird is ill.*

and is not distressed by being weighed, then check its weight and write this down. During veterinary treatment and when recovering from some illnesses, your vet may suggest you keep a daily check on your bird's weight. If you think your bird is ill, you should act without any delay in order to save it or prevent it getting worse. By the time a bird appears to be off color you can be sure that it is very ill indeed, so always act promptly.

traveling to the office. It is important to make sure you minimize stressful situations when handling a sick bird. Stress alone can make things much worse for the bird. Act in a calm, confident manner and keep your bird somewhere with subdued lighting. Ensure that you restrict the bird's ability to see out of its carrier during traveling as this also helps to reduce stress.

Below: *This bird can move in and out of heat from the infrared lamp as it wishes.*

VITAL HEAT TREATMENT

Sick birds usually gain great benefit from simply being put somewhere very warm, around 80 to 86°F (27 to 30°C) and kept in subdued light. The best way to supply heat is via a ceramic infrared heat lamp placed above the cage. This emits heat only and no light. This should be placed so the bird can move away from the lamp if at any time it feels too hot. Use a thermometer to check the temperature around the cage (but keep this out of reach of the bird). The provision of heat will mean the bird will need to drink regularly, so make sure the bird has easy access to drinking water and wet foods, such as grapes or apples. Once the bird is receiving this heat treatment, phone your vet, explain the bird's symptoms and get emergency advice without any delay. Be prepared to take your bird to the vet. When doing so, keep it very warm all the time it is

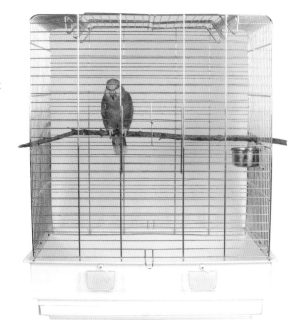

First aid checklist

Older birds are prone to overgrown claws.

With its long claws filed down, this bird perches more comfortably.

STOPPING BLEEDING

Very small bleeding wounds, including claws clipped too short, usually cease bleeding within a few minutes, so you may not need to intervene, other than to make sure the bird remains calm and moves as little as possible. More serious bleeding will need to be treated. You will need to restrain the bird by holding it in a towel. Try to get the bird to remain relaxed; keeping the bird's

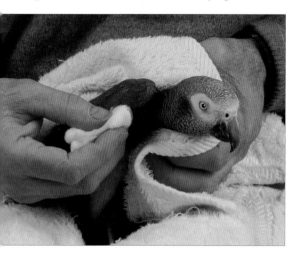

Above: *Always act calmly and confidently when treating a bird. It will sense this and be less stressed.*

Above left and right: *Overgrown claws can cause a bird problems when perching and climbing. If dealing with very long claws, don't cut them back all at once. Cut (or preferably file) a little off over a few days.*

head covered with part of the towel usually ensures this. To stop bleeding on hard parts of the bird only (the claws or beak), use a styptic pencil, which you can get from your vet. This is used by dipping it in water before applying it to the point of bleeding on the bird. To stop bleeding on other parts, use a cotton ball on the wound and apply firm but not excessive pressure. Bleeding should stop within two to three minutes. Remove the cotton ball gently and be careful when handling the bird so as not to restart the bleeding.

CHECKLIST

Below is a checklist of some things to keep for your bird's first-aid needs. However, unless you are an experienced bird-keeper, you should seek advice from a specialist avian vet before treating your bird at home. Always keep your specialist avian vet's phone numbers and contact details handy.

First aid

Items that you can get from a bird vet or a pharmacy:
- Cotton balls and cotton swabs, used to help stop bleeding
- Glucose powder, used diluted at 2 teaspoons per 1 pint (10 ml/570 ml) of water to administer essential fluids and basic nutrition in

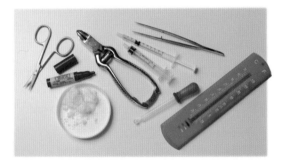

an emergency, when a bird has difficulty feeding on normal food
- A styptic pencil to stop bleeding of claws or beak only
- Avian antibiotic ointment to apply to small skin wounds
- Thermometer, used to measure the air temperature (not to measure the bird's temperature)
- Small syringes for giving food or medicine.
- Forceps
- Pair of clippers

Items that you can get from a bird-supplements supplier:
- Avian antiseptic to clean items that the bird comes into contact with, such as syringes, feeding spoons, feed bowls, etc.
- Electrolyte/probiotic solution. Used as a tonic to aid digestion and after other medication (such as antibiotics) has ceased being given
- Avian disinfectant to clean cages, aviaries and perches
- Avian multivitamin powder to ensure that birds (especially sick birds or those on a poor diet) are getting all the essential vitamins and minerals
- Ceramic infrared heat lamp or hospital cage to keep a sick bird at a raised temperature to aid recovery
- Traveling cage with one low-level, securely fitted perch
- Hand-feeding food to be given to a sick bird as a warm and fairly thick liquid food by means of a syringe or bent spoon to ensure adequate levels of nutrition

Household items:
- Towel for holding a bird when necessary, such as when administering medication. Towels should be of a neutral or pale color, such as white, cream or pale green. Dark-colored towels may frighten the bird.

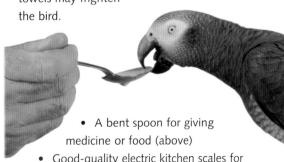

- A bent spoon for giving medicine or food (above)
- Good-quality electric kitchen scales for keeping a check on a sick bird's weight
- Pair of small, sharp scissors

Index

Note: Page numbers set in *italics* indicate a reference to a picture caption; page numbers set in **bold** type indicate a main text entry.

A

African brown-headed parrot *12*
African gray parrot 9, 11, 20, 22, *23*, 24, **29**, *29*, 36, *36*, 38, *42*, 48, 53, *53*, 56, 57, 58, 80, 84, *84*, 86, 87, 88, 90, 95, 104, *105, 109*, 110, *115*
Amazon parrot 9, 19, 20, 23, 24, **26–7**, 30, 36, 38, 57, 58, 79, 80, 84, *84, 85, 85*, 86, 87, 88, 90, 95, 110
blue-fronted 26, *27*
mealy *13*
orange-winged *25*, 26, *27*
red-lored 26
yellow-naped *26, 99*
ageing 25
aggression 6, 8, 9, 25, 26, 28, 30, 34, 37, 41, 56, 64, 100, **112–3**, *112*, 117
anesthesia 122
applied behavior analysis 47, **48–9**, **50–1, 52–3**, 64
aviaries 12, 30, 32, 79, 104
indoor 30, 84–5
outdoor 30, **90–1**, *90, 91*, 100, 107
planting in **90–1**

B

baby birds 36–7, *36, 37,* **38–9**, *38, 39*, 46
bars, cage **86**, 88
bathing 13
beaks 15, *15*, 16, *16*, 18, 20, *20*, 21, 22–3, 26, 30–1, 76, 101, 124
clicking 58
grinding 59
behavior, juvenile **36–7**
biting *22*, 23, 25, 28, 31, 48, 50, *50*, 51, 53, *73*, 98, **112–3**, *112, 113*
bleeding, dealing with 124
bonding 24, 28, 32, 33, 34, 69, 75, 99, 104, 106, 116–7, *117*
box, roosting 32, **88**, *88*, 100, 115, 116
budgerigars 8, 9, 20, 26, 32, **35**, *35, 38*, 47, 80

C

cages 11, 12, 24, 30, 31, 32, 33, *39*, 44–5, 54, 60, 62, 64, 70, 71, 78, **84–5**, *84, 85*, 86–7, 88–9, *98*, 100, 101, 104, 106, 113, 114, 116
traveling *see* carriers
caiques **33**
black-headed *33*
carriers 44, *44*, 91
chewing *23*, *23*, 98, **101, 116–7**, *116*
chicks 21
claws 25, 124, *124*
clicker training **52–3**, *53*
climbing 15, 18, 86, 99

cockatiels 8, 19, 20, 26, **35**, *35*, 80, 84, 90, 93, 95
cockatoos 9, *9, 16*, 17, 19, 20, 22, *22*, 23, 24, 26, **28**, 36, 41, 58, *58, 82, 84*, 85, *86*, 90, *92*, 93, 104, 110, 114
citron-crested *104*
Goffin's 28
Major Mitchell's *29, 36*
Moluccan 28, *106*
sulfur-crested 28, *62*
umbrella *28*
commands in training 24, 35, 41, 61, **64–5**
drop it **77**, *77*
go 64, **72–3**, *72, 73*
go down 45, 61, 64, 65, *66, 68*, 69, 78
off there 64, **74–5**
on here 64, **75**, *75*
stay 64, **70–1**, *70, 72, 73*
step up 48, **50–1, 50, 51**, 52, 53, **54–5**, 61, 62, 64, **66**, *67*, **68–9**, *68, 69*, 101, 113, *113*, 120
take this **76**, *76*
commencement signals 59
Congo gray *see* African gray
conures 18, 26, **31**, 32, 36, *85*
blue-crowned 31
golden-capped 31, *31*
green-cheeked 31
maroon-bellied 31
Patagonian 31
sun 31, *31*
corella, little 28
crash landings 10, 43, 45, *102, 103*, 108

D

desensitizing 103
destructiveness 6, 25, 30, 98, **116–7**
diet *23*, 34, 45, **92–7**
changing **96–7**, *97*
digestion 21, *21*

E

eclectus parrot *23*, **34**, *42*, 47
red-sided *34*
escape reflex 10, 102
escaped birds **118–21**, *118, 119, 120, 121*
eyes 43, *56*, 58
pinning 57, *57, 58*

F

feathers 13, *16*, 17, *17*, **18–9**, *18, 19*, **25**, 34, *42, 42*, 43, 56, *56*, 59, *59*, 72, 87, 105, *109*
plucking 6, 25, 28, 29, 34, 41, 42, 98, **104–7**, *104, 105*
repair of 105, **110–1**, *111*
feeding habits 12, *12*, **20–1**, 32
feet 15, 20, *20*, 25, 43, *43*, 86–7, *87*
flights, day *see* aviaries
flying **10–1**, *10*, 12, 14, 16, *17*, 20, 43, **45**, 48, 64, 70, 71, 72–3, 74–5, 104, 108, 110, 118, *119*
foods 49, *49*, 60, *60*, 93, 94, 95, 107
dangerous 96
food-begging 46, *46*
food pots 45, 86, 87, 89, 91

Index

G

galah *11, 13, 28, 104*
gliding 47, *47*
greeting posture 58–9
grills, floor 86

H

hand-reared birds 28,
　36–7, *37*, 104, 116–7
harnesses **79**
hawk-headed parrot 27
health checks **42–3**, *42,*
　43, 122, *122*
hearing 11
heartbeat 16, 110
heat treatment 123, *123*

I

imping damaged wing
　feathers 110–1, *110–1*
imprinting 37
insurance, veterinary *25*

J

Jardine's parrot 22, 33

L

language 6–7, **8–9, 56,**
　56
　body **50, 56–9**
　calls 6, 22, 35, 56, 59,
　114, *114*
　lifespan **24–5**
lorikeet, rainbow *12*
lovebirds 19, 26, 33, **34**
　Fischer's *34*

M

macaws 14, 19, 20, 22,
　22, 23, 24, 26, **30–1**,
　36, 39, 41, 57, 58, *58*,
　85, 86, *90*, 95, 104,
　110

blue and gold 6, *24*,
　30, *30, 39, 58*, 85
green-winged 8, 30,
　30, 85
Hahn's 30
hyacinth *15, 56*, 98
scarlet *6, 18*, 30, *30*,
　85, 99, *41*
yellow-collared 30
maturity rates 36
Meyer's parrot *18*, 22,
　24, *24*, 33, *46, 52, 53*,
　57, 65, 76, 84, *84*, 88,
　95, *109*
mimicry 29, 32, 33, **80–1**,
　80, *81, 115*, 117
minerals 12, *13*, 95
model-rival teaching
　method **82–3**
molting 19, 110, **111**
muscles **16–7**, *16, 17*

N

nervousness 6, 25, 28, 29,
　41, 54, 55, 56, 60, *61*,
　62–3, 64, 86, 98, **102–3**
nesting holes 17
noise **22**, 25, 29, 33, 34,
　41, 98
nutritional values of foods
　93, 94

P

parakeets 26, **32**
　Bourke's 32
　grass 93
　kakariki 32
　quaker *37*
　ring-necked *20*, 32,
　32, 114
　rosella 32, *32*, 87
　turquoise 32
parrotlets 14, **33**
　Mexican *33*

Pavlov, Ivan 47
Pepperberg, Irene 82–3,
　83
perches 44, *44, 45*, 54,
　62, 64, *72*, **86–7**, *87*,
　89, 90, 91, *91*, 101,
　116, 122
　stick 68, *68*, 112
pionus parrot 22, *27*
　blue-headed *13*
　bronze-winged 27
　Maximilian's 27
　red-vented 27
poicephalus parrot 22,
　33, 36, 57
preening 13, 15, 19, *48*
　mutual 59, **100**
punishment 61, 106

R

rescue centers 40
restraint **78–9**, *78, 79*,
　124
rewards **49**, 51, *51*, 52,
　52, 53, *53*, 54, 55, *55*,
　61, 62, *63*, 64–5, 66,
　66, 67, *67*, 69, 70, *70*,
　71, 73, 74, 75, *75*, 76,
　78, *78*

S

screaming 6, 26, 28, 37,
　114–5
Senegal parrot 22, 24,
　33, 57, 90
shoulder sitting 73,
　112–3, 113
showering 13, 19, 107,
　107
sight 10–11, 15
skeleton **14–5**, *14*
Skinner, B.F. 47
spraying *see* showering
stands 24, 89, 101

stand-trained birds 70
swing feeders 86, *86*

T

tail fanning 58
talking 6, 26, 29, 30, 32,
　33, 35, **80–1**, *81*,
　82–3, 117
taming 62–3
Timneh gray parrot *15*,
　20, 22, **29**, *29*, 48, 50,
　53, 58, *71, 75*, 80, *121*
toilet training **101**
toweling 44, 78–9, *79*,
　122, 125
toys 23, *24*, 33, 45, 52,
　60, 65, *65*, 75, 76, *76*,
　88–9, *88, 89*, 100,
　101, 107, 115, *115*,
　116, *116*
treats *61*, 62, 63, *63*, 65,
　75, 76, 101

V

vets, avian 122, 123, 124

W

walking 16, *17*
water, drinking 12, *13*
water pots 87, 91
wing-clipping 6, 10, *42*,
　43, 45, 60–1, *72*, 91,
　102, 104, **108–9**, *109*,
　111
wingspan 84, *84*

Y

young birds 60

Picture credits

Unless otherwise credited below, all the photographs in this book were taken by **Neil Sutherland** for Interpet Publishing. The publishers would also like to thank Mike Taylor at **Northern Parrots** (www.24Parrot.com) for kindly supplying the pictures of cages and cage furnishings that are credited below. The credits for the inset pictures on pages 1–3 number the images from left to right on their appropriate pages.

Jane Burton, Warren Photographic:
30 top right, 60–1.
Philip de Ste. Croix: 106 center.
Greg Glendell: 104 top, 119 bottom right, 121 top left.
Interpet Ltd: 89 top right.
iStockphoto.com:
Roberto Adrian: 22 left.
Robert Ahrens: 11 left.
Cynthia Baldauf: 121 bottom right.
Stacy Barnett: 14 (inset et seq), 22 (inset et seq), 112 left.
Vera Bogaerts: 91.
Alex Bramwell: 30 bottom left.
Emily Bristor: 31 right.
Patrick Bronson: 6.
Sandra Dunlap: 30 bottom right.
Lisa Eastman: 23 top.
eROMAZe: 37 bottom right.
EuToch: 4–5 (inset 4).
Dany Farina: 40 bottom.
Lee Feldstein: 1 (inset 1), 2–3 (inset 1), 4–5 (inset 6), 28 bottom center, 30 (inset), 36 top right, 37 bottom left, 41 right, 42 top right, 109 right.
Susan Flashman: 32 top center.
Micha Fleuren: 28 (inset).
Nicola Gavin: 48 bottom left, 82 bottom left.
Steve Geer: 35 top, 42 center left.
Joanne Green: 86 left.
Andrew Howe: 47 bottom right.

Eric Isselée: 2–3 (inset 5), 6 (inset).
Kevdog818: 16 top.
Kerstin Klaassen: 36 (inset et seq).
Jill Lang: 4–5 (inset 8), 27 top left, 37 top right, 39 top left & right, 40 left.
Mandygodbehear: 81 bottom right.
Sue McDonald: 32 bottom left, 47 bottom left.
Vasko Miokovic: 103 top.
Jim Mires: 46 (inset et seq).
Eli Mordechai: 58 left.
Mval: 85 top right.
Nancy Nehring: 8 (inset et seq).
Giacomo Nodari: 2–3 (inset 7), 60 (inset et seq).
Joanne Pecha: 1 (inset 3).
Dmitry Pichugin: 34 top.
Pixonaut: 18 top left.
Jan Rihak: 119 top.
Malcolm Romain: 118 bottom.
Ronen: 24 bottom left.
SkyCreative: 34 bottom left.
Laurie L Snidow: 56 top.
Eline Spek: 34 (inset).
Tyler Stalman: 102 top.
Douglas Stetner: 32 top.
Susan Stewart: 62.
Mark Stout: 2–3 (inset 3).
Ashley Whitworth: 34 bottom center.
Lisa F Young: 41 top.
Frank Lane Picture Agency/flpa-images.co.uk: 8 (Frans Lanting/Minden Pictures), 10 (Jurgen and Christine Sohns), 13 left (Mitsuaki Iwago/Minden Pictures), 13 right (Frans Lanting/Minden Pictures), 26 top right (Jurgen and Christine Sohns), 27 bottom center (Pete Oxford/Minden Pictures), 27 bottom right (David Hosking), 33 top center (David Hosking), 98 top right (Pete Oxford/Minden Pictures), 99 top (Jurgen and Christine Sohns), 99 bottom (Frans Lanting/Minden Pictures).

Northern Parrots: 44 top center, 84 top center, 85 bottom left and center, 86 top, 88 bottom left, 89 top left & center, 98 bottom center.
Professor Irene Pepperberg, The Alex Foundation: 83 top, 83 bottom (with thanks to Arlene Levin-Rowe).
Shutterstock Inc:
John Austin: 12 top.
Stacy Barnett: 58 top.
Kevin Britland: 33 bottom.
Katrina Brown: 35 bottom, 39 bottom center.
Stephen Coburn: 120 top.
Judy Crawford: 114.
Steve Cukrov: 26 left.
Demark: 38 bottom right.
Joe Gough: 11 right.
Joanne Harris and Daniel Bubnich: 32 top right, 39 bottom left, 39 bottom right.
Kasia: 15 top left.
Lancelot and Naelle: 90.
Jill Lang: 36 left.
Tan Yoke Liang: 18 bottom right.
Adrian Lindley 92.
Jasenka Luksa: 52–3 top.
Lori Martin: 4–5 (inset 2).
Holger Mette: 9.
Debbie Oetgen: 28 top.
James Doss: 98 (inset et seq).
SGC: 7, 118 (inset et seq).
Mark E. Stout: 31 left.
Nick Stubbs: 46 bottom.
Sword Serenity: 28 bottom right, 97 bottom.
Morozova Tatiana: 87 top right.
Ivan Tihelka: 87 bottom.
Tihis: 20 bottom left.
Nathalie Speliers Ufermann: 26 (inset).
Gert Johannes Jacobus Very: 12 bottom.
Elena Yakusheva: 37 top left.